Indexing It All

History and Foundations of Information Science
Edited by Michael Buckland, Jonathan Furner, and Markus Krajewski

Human Information Retrieval by Julian Warner

Good Faith Collaboration: The Culture of Wikipedia by Joseph Michael Reagle Jr.

Paper Machines: About Cards & Catalogs, 1548–1929 by Markus Krajewski, translated by Peter Krapp

Information and Intrigue: From Index Cards to Dewey Decimals to Alger Hiss by Colin B. Burke

Indexing It All: The Subject in the Age of Documentation, Information, and Data by Ronald E. Day

Indexing It All

The Subject in the Age of Documentation, Information, and Data

Ronald E. Day

The MIT Press
Cambridge, Massachusetts
London, England

MIT Press books may be purchased at special quantity discounts for business or sales promotional use. For information, please email special_sales@mitpress.mit.edu.

This book was set in Stone by the MIT Press. Printed and bound in the United States of America.

Library of Congress Cataloging-in-Publication Data is available.
ISBN: 978-0-262-02821-9

10 9 8 7 6 5 4 3 2 1

Dedication: *Once again, in admiration and friendship*

Contents

Preface

Indexing It All: The Subject in the Age of Documentation, Information, and Data, gives a critical epistemic-historical account of the development of the modern documentary tradition and its mode of governmentality in the twentieth century and now the twenty-first. In these pages I argue that documentary indexing and indexicality play a major and increasing role in organizing personal and social identity and value and in reorganizing social and political life. This phenomenon has resulted in a rewriting of personal and social psychologies of the Western tradition of the past two hundred years, and it is altering notions of self and personhood, texts and textuality, and personal judgment and the role of critique in thought and politics. Today those foundations of Enlightenment thought, such as individual natural powers, freedom from surveillance, and the rights of speech, are routinely overrun and erased with the important aid of documentary systems in the service of state and corporate power and profit, in both democratic and nondemocratic states. Routinely and obsessively we use online resources—whose algorithms and indexes both serve and profit from us in ways that the users are largely unaware—as the way of overcoming the physical and emotional distances that are a consequence of modernity, and in particular capitalist modernity, where markets have become the means and the ends for reasoning, communication, and increasingly, emotion. These devices have become the governance structures—the "idea" or "concept"—for our human manner of being (subsuming other beings in this, as well), which increasingly subsume and subvert the former roles of personal judgment and critique in personal and social being and politics.

In writing *Indexing It All* as a critical epistemic-historical account of these events in twentieth- and twenty-first-century modernity, I intend to show the historical continuity of documentary techniques and technologies, which extend through documentation, information, and data and their sciences and runs through pre-computational and computational techniques and technologies. This book is an intellectual history of the modern role of documentary indexing—documentary social, psychological, and political positioning—and how such has shaped and continues to shape what the mid-twentieth-century French documentalist Suzanne Briet termed "homo documentator" (Briet 2006)—documentary man—in the "information age." (I have more inclusively used "the modern documentary tradition" in this book for the term "information age.")

Critical works, such as this book, attempt to bear witness to some event and to intervene in such. This book does both. We bear witness to the reality, violence, stories, and told and untold truths of events and to our own self-positioning and agency within these as best as we can reckon. We bear witness to the idea and image of an age and society and also attempt to intervene in such. By presenting the modern documentary tradition in terms of Hegelian dialectic in this work, I attempt to intervene through analytical and historical critique in the unfolding of the idea of an "information age" and "information society" that extends through a modern documentary episteme. In this book, by inversion, I give a critique of standard information age historiographies which broadly circulate in popular culture and even in scholarship (made up of celebration, endless optimism, works of individual genius, and the paradoxical eternal present in the invention of the technologically "new"). The narrative gives an account that attempts to connect the dots between usually separate traditions and explain the state of the documentary subject that we now find in late modern technological societies.

We live as social creatures and creatures of habit but with radical potentials. That radicalness is foundational for human beings. Though this book is rather dark in its vision upon its topic, it claims to constitute but one light upon the matter, and a light that is little shone.[1] I hold with great admiration and affection libraries, archives, and other so-called documentary institutions and their at least three-thousand-year traditions. Without them, their professionals, and their traditions of service and duty, civilizations would not exist, and in their absence civilizations have fallen. This is not a minor observation or event, and I can't stress strongly enough, especially today in the face of their corporate takeover and replacement, the values of such public institutions. And, of course, the advent of the Internet and its technologies during my lifetime has brought about a wealth and accessibility of texts and knowledge that was unthinkable when I grew up; I have benefited greatly and hold with admiration this practical miracle and the work of the people and institutions that have contributed to this. But, at the same time, what these institutions and virtual sites have held and hold are texts of various natures, and it is in the reading of these texts, as texts, that the powers of any individual, group, or civilization appears and being is determined.

Documentary systems as widely deployed and accepted means, measures, and representations of beings and texts are a rather modern phenomenon, appearing only since the late eighteenth century. In the last century and a half these have gained an increasing foothold in creating and mediating both documentary subjects and objects according to an epistemology of representation, correspondence, and mutual abstraction and reduction. This is what I mean when I refer to the *modern documentary tradition*. Thinking through this tradition as a defining concept for being, knowledge, and governance in our modern age is what this book attempts to do.

Acknowledgments

This book wouldn't have been possible without the resources, suggestions, and corrections of a number of people. I would like to thank, in particular: Karl F. MacDorman and Selma Šabanović for sharing their knowledge and expertise in android and robotic sciences, and Karl for his very generous and expert review and corrections of the chapter of this book that discusses androids and the uncanny valley; Michael Buckland for his (as usual) exemplary work, this time in reading, comments, and corrections of the entire manuscript, and in particular those sections of the book that discuss the transition in library and information science from documentation to information science; and of course, for introducing me to the work of Suzanne Briet many years ago and for his always generous support and inspiration; Lai Ma for her dissertation and for working with me, which led me to think more carefully about Michael Buckland's work among other things in this book; Neal Thomas of the University of North Carolina, whose brilliant work informs the core elements of the chapter on social computing and which helped me think about information needs more carefully than before; Mary L. Gray, who invited me to Microsoft Research in New England in order to talk about this book project and so kept this project alive when I thought otherwise. I am very grateful to Margy Avery at MIT Press, who made a great effort to hear my talk on the manuscript of this book and who accepted the book for publication and who, along with Katie Persons and Marcy Ross, to whom I am also grateful, saw it through publication. I also very much thank Mary Bagg for her careful and insightful copyediting; the book is considerably improved because of her. And, my thanks go to the anonymous readers who reviewed the initial manuscript. An earlier version of part of the chapter on citation indexing in this book appears in Blaise

Cronin and Cassidy Sugimoto's *Beyond Bibliometrics: Harnessing Multidimensional Indicators of Scholarly Impact* (MIT Press, 2014). The initial draft of this book was written during a one semester sabbatical from Indiana University, Bloomington. My thanks to Jiangmei and Dexter for giving me the time to work on this book.

1 Introduction

This definition [of documentation as evidence] has often been countered by linguists and philosophers, who are necessarily infatuated with minutia and logic. Thanks to their analysis of the content of this idea, one can propose here a definition, which may be, at the present time, the most accurate, but is also the most abstract, and thus, the least accessible: "any concrete or symbolic indexical sign [*indice*], preserved or recorded toward the ends of representing, of reconstituting, or of proving a physical or intellectual phenomenon. …

Still, the tools of intellectual work have deeply transformed the attitude of the scholar, whatever may be his specialty. The factors of space and time intervene much more than in the past. The date-book, the telephone, the microfilm reader, the typewriter, the dictaphone, and the teletype give to intellectual work a *different rhythm*. …

"Homo documentator" is born out of new conditions of research and technique [*technique*].
—Suzanne Briet, *Qu'est-ce que la documentation?/What Is Documentation?* (1951/2006)

As I did in my earlier book, *The Modern Invention of Information: Discourse, History, and Power* (Day 2001), in this book I examine information as a cultural and social phenomenon, and I do so at a particular historical moment. In that earlier book I gave a critical, conceptual history of the dominant understanding of "information" in modernity—that is, as seemingly auto-affective (i.e., as "facts" or what in deconstruction was called "presence") and an immediately useful unitary body of meaningful signs—starting from European documentation in the beginning of the twentieth century and reaching up until the 1990s discourse on "the virtual." I wrote that book as a critical intervention into the hyper-inflated discourses of "information," the "information age," and the "information society" during the dot-com era, when an inflated discourse in ordinary and media language about information was a primary driver in financial and housing speculation, education reform, and the further erosion of an industrial working class in the United States following the years of the U.S. presidents Reagan and George H. W. Bush. This was the Clinton era of deregulation, financial speculation, and adulation for a class of so-called symbolic analysts—in the words of Robert Reich (1992), who served as President Clinton's Secretary of Labor—especially in the speculative financial industry and in the information industry, which came to replace industrial production as a dominant source for wealth in the United States.

This book, *Indexing It All*, continues that investigation, though it now extrapolates, greatly expands, and contemporizes the concept of "index" introduced in my earlier work in connection with the way the French documentalist Suzanne Briet used the term in *Qu'est-ce que la documentation?* (Briet 1951), translated and published as *What Is Documentation?* (Briet 2006). The focus upon the documentary index (understood as a mode of social positioning) in this present book encompasses the twentieth- and early twenty-first-century tradition of documentation, information, and data and their sciences (what I call "the modern documentary tradition"). Through a critical epistemic-historical method this book examines the notions and uses of indexicality, from documental through informational and into data moments of a documentary "episteme." (Here I use Michel Foucault's term for historical periods when central discursive and technical devices orient understanding and production, and society and culture, as well as technological innovations, techniques, and methods in certain directions rather than others.) The book examines the transition of indexes from being explicit professional structures that mediate the relation of user needs and documentary information in seeking, searching, and retrieving to being implicit infrastructural devices in everyday information and communication acts. And, given this transition, *Indexing It All* follows the increasing representation of individuals and groups in the forms of documents, information, and then data.

My approach in this book, as in my earlier one, is to examine conceptual cases that cover the historical period of later modernity, from the early twentieth century to the present time—beginning with documentation's user-document distinction, and reaching up to the mediation of this relation through the logical tools of information retrieval and social networking, and then to the subsumption of both documents and users as data.

Hegelian dialectic in the book provides a way of understanding the three moments of the modern documentary tradition as a coherent tradition with a continuum of changing (but consistent and overlapping) technologies, techniques, and epistemic assumptions. Dialectics, I will argue, inhabits not only the major historical moments of the modern documentary tradition, but it does so because the sociotechnical logic of the user-documentation relationship is fundamentally dialectical. In the era of post–World War II information science, this starts to take the form of a cybernetic or feedback systems orientation, which expands to being a socially wide "knowledge management" system of governmentality, which in turn serves the larger ends of democratic-capitalist political economies in the valorization of the paradox of an ideologically controlled or "liberal" notion of individual freedom. (See, for example, Norbert Wiener's *The Human Use of Human Beings* (1954), a discourse on the role of cybernetic control in democracy.) In this, subjectivity is mediated as expressive forms in information, knowledge, and communication activities. More recently, the discourse of "data," conceived as a form of auto-affective presence or "fact," has come to supersede the trope of "information."

Hegelian dialectic nicely shows the historical "progress" of modern knowledge in the modern documentary tradition: from the first logical-historical moment of a difference between person and text (the moment of a relatively independent subject and object); to the second moment of representation and the mediation of the two, through notions of "aboutness" (i.e., information and information needs), leading to users and documents; to the third moment, the final completion of the modern documentary tradition in the "uplifting" and subsumption (*Aufhebung*) of both the subject and the object to become a subjective/objective synthesis as "data."

While some readers may immediately reject a Hegelian reading of the modern documentary tradition, I would argue that perhaps we have not understood strongly enough the continuity of logic and power in this tradition and its progressive and overlapping forms of science (documentation, information science, and data science). A more cohesive analysis across a variety of what may at first appear as disparate disciplines and cases may offer a more coherent understanding of a modern documentary tradition.

Documentary notions of representation occur through notions of evidence or "aboutness," which transform the possibility of identity into the empirical reality of what deconstruction termed "presence," or what Paul

Otlet in his works called "facts." As in the distant past, but increasingly and exponentially throughout the twentieth century and up until today, such "facts" occur through the infrastructuralization of documentary techniques and technologies not only into scientific and professional activities, but also as mediating devices in everyday life. With increasing recursivity, scale, and ubiquity in sociotechnical infrastructures, algorithms and indexes have become both more opaque and more mobile, hiding the logical and psychological assumptions that once were very clear in traditional top-down and universal classification and taxonomic structures, as well as in other professional information techniques and technologies.

Increasingly, for example, search algorithms have changed from being obvious professional devices to being transparent or everyday sociocultural or even physical codes through which one must pass to gain knowledge and to become an active and mature person in society. (To use a very simple example, most of the younger generations in modernized countries have acquired everyday information retrieval skills that were only twenty years ago the sole possession of librarians and other information professionals; they have also acquired expectations of information quantity and accessibility that would have been unimaginable for ordinary people even twenty years ago.) We live in a world of codes through which we routinely consciously and unconsciously pass, rather than through transcendental and rather complicated professional devices (Deleuze 1995). These codes are not only cognitive, but also increasingly are expressed by the body itself. What Foucault called the "disciplinary society" is now introjected into the foundations of expressions and the body; documentary codes—evidence of our being x or having y knowledge and skills—form the unconscious and so structure our expressions. This book gives one reading of this journey of consciousness, not only as it is "mediated," but even more so as it is shaped in its very social and personal identity, through documentary tools, forms, and infrastructures of expression and meaning.

Recently in many critical works regarding the Internet—for example, in Tiziana Terranova's *Network Culture* (2004)—there has been expressed the hope that the Internet represents a platform for something other than dialectic, for the emergence of a Deleuzian or Negrian "multitude" of singularities that can escape a dialectical logic for political economy, and with this, also escape the priority of the notion of the subject within Western culture. My argument in this book doesn't disagree with this hope, but rather I suggest that new media information and data systems may not have so quickly broken from the logical forms that characterize documentation systems or from the pressures and attractors of sociopolitical structures based on the privilege of the subject. In contrast to much of the more hopeful literature on "new media," I must admit that this is a somewhat darker book.

Documents and Indexes

At this point, in the way of a further introduction to the following chapters, let us ask: What are documents and what are indexes?

The concept of the document during the twentieth century has been conceptually, empirically, and grammatically multiple and entangled (Lund 2009). Both because it has been an important traditional definition of the term "document" in library and information science (and before that, in European documentation), and because it often carries the same normative meaning in everyday discourse and dictionary definitions, we will consider throughout this book the dominant modern sense of the term "document" in the modern documentary tradition to be that of "evidence" (Buckland 1997). And consequently, after Buckland (1997) again, let us take it is as a prima facie understanding that documents can be any type of ontological substance that acts as evidence. This is not to say that evidence is what documents (or information) *are*, of course (the term "document" refers to nominal, rather than real, kinds of entities), but it is one of the most important and normative definitions of "document" in recent and contemporary modernity.

There is, however, circularity to the notion of documents as being evidence, which begs the question of what it is that documents are evidence of. All evidence is evidence *of* something, and that something belongs to orders of possible evidence for a need (from which the need is formed). Documents as evidence are ontological entities whose evidentiary origins lie in their belonging to taxonomic or indexical regimes or to looser discursive or conversational regimes. They are meaningful signs in relation to other signs, linguistic or otherwise, within whose difference from one another and in relation to things and events they gain their identity and their referentiality. From these signs—as cultural forms and in social norms of performance—information or knowledge needs are formed and answered. We cannot ask for what is not known, so we satisfy our needs by choosing among available options of what looks best to us. Needs are formed from signs as signifiers of things that can help focus and accomplish tasks and desires.[1]

The totality of these signs may be theoretically finite or practically infinite. They may exist as formal taxonomies (now often called "ontologies" in information science) or they may exist as informal senses of difference or distinction within linguistic grammars, discourses, and conversations. They may exist as products of professional and other scientific classificatory or cataloging practices (in zoology or library science, for example) or they may be products of informal assumptions and customs (Bowker and Star 1999). They may be formally a priori or they may be judgments expressed "on the fly" and reinforced as cultural and social assumptions by habits of practice (as with prejudices and other "pre-judgments").

Indeed, even professional, a priori, taxonomies rely upon use to keep them present and available, and so they all exist one way or another as what Ferdinand de Saussure termed *langue*: hypothetical or actual fields of potential meaningful actions through which meaningful speech acts occur. (Speech acts also, however, continually reestablish *langue* through their performance.) Such speech acts are treated in the modern documentary tradition as "self-evident" evidence (once again, using Derridean vocabulary, as auto-affective "presence"). But there is nothing self-evident about evidence. Evidence is evidence only within contexts of what may be considered to be evidential. And while these abstract forms may be hypothetical as a set, they are nevertheless real and established as part of a real set or *langue* in their continual performance. English or ideology or a person's knowledge are hypothetical sets of real potentialities that are established as substantive actual entities and sets of entities through their repeated actualization in meaningful acts of expression. There isn't any separate Platonic realm of "ideas" apart from their enunciations, but these ideas nonetheless exist as potentially actualized cultural forms and social norms.

The place of documents in taxonomies and discourses, as signifying forms that are *about* something, means that documents are signs that have referential relations to other signs and to forms of life. As John Seely Brown and Paul Duguid (2000) put it, there is a "social life of information"—documents do meaningful things because they are meaningful within networks and uses of other meaningful signs (which may be linguistic, physical, visual, or otherwise). In their circulation in such networks and uses they both point to other signs, both in and outside of their networks of circulation, and they trace their social and practical networks as a whole. They are, in this way, what I earlier called as a certain form of quasi-objects, "informational objects"; they inform or reference something, but viewed critically, they also inform us about how they reference, namely by tracing the living networks and economies of signs that they circulate within (Day 2001).

At the start of *Qu'est-ce que la documentation?* (*What Is Documentation?*), the mid-twentieth-century French librarian and documentalist Suzanne Briet used the term *indice* to name documentary signs (Briet 1951; Briet 2006). In her text, the term *indice* may be translated into English as "sign" (here I use *indice* for both the singular and plural form of the word to avoid confusion with the plural "indices" in English). But it should be pointed out that the word "sign" in French is *signe*. *Indice* is a particular type of sign, namely that of being an "indexical sign." Indexical signs both reference a thing and gather together a universe of signification for the purpose of that referencing. For example, back-of-the-book indexes reference important terms within a book's content and in so doing not only give the term meaning in terms of the book's content, but they also help to position that book within a larger discursive field. The difference between a good human-generated index of a book and a bad machine-generated index of a book involves the ability to create an index that positions the first set of references within the meaning and sense of the second. A term is meaningful within the book only because the book is meaningful within a field of discourse. The best indexes are not just machine-made, but are human-made by experts that understand not only the page or the documentation referents of the indexical terms, but also the universe of meaning and sense that makes some of the document's terms more important than others and gives them certain meanings and sense. Human indexes are what machine algorithms strive toward by the use of various syntactical and semantic techniques and technologies.

Here I quote from the beginning pages of Suzanne Briet's text in which she discusses documents, evidence, and *indice*:

From the very beginning, Latin culture and its heritage have given to the word *document* the meaning of instruction or proof. RICHELET's dictionary, just as LITTRÉ's, are two French sources that bear witness to this. A contemporary bibliographer concerned about clarity has put forth this brief definition: "A document is a proof in support of a fact."

If one refers to the "official" definitions of the French Union of Documentation Organizations [l'Union française des organismes de documentation], one ascertains that the document is defined as: "all bases of materially fixed knowledge, and capable of being used for consultation, study, and proof."

This definition has often been countered by linguists and philosophers, who are, as they should be, infatuated with minutia and logic. Thanks to their analysis of the content of this idea, one can propose here a definition, which may be, at the present time, the most accurate, but is also the most abstract, and thus, the least accessible: "any concrete or symbolic indexical sign [indice], preserved or recorded toward the ends of representing, of reconstituting, or of proving a physical or intellectual phenomenon."

Is a star a document? Is a pebble rolled by a torrent a document? Is a living animal a document? No. But the photographs and the catalogs of stars, the stones in a museum of mineralogy, and the animals that are cataloged and shown in a zoo, are documents.

In our age of multiple and accelerated broadcasts, the least event, scientific or political, once it has been brought into public knowledge, immediately becomes weighted down under a "veil of documents" ([to quote the philosopher] Raymond BAYER). Let us admire the documentary fertility of a simple originary fact: for example, an antelope of a new kind has been encountered in Africa by an explorer who has succeeded in capturing an individual that is then brought back to Europe for our Botanical Garden [Jardin des plantes]. A press release makes the event known by newspaper, by radio, and by newsreels. The discovery becomes the topic of an announcement at the Academy of Sciences. A professor of the Museum discusses it in his courses. The living animal is placed in a cage and cataloged (zoological garden). Once it is dead, it will be stuffed and preserved (in the Museum). It is loaned to an Exposition. It is played on a soundtrack at the cinema. Its voice is recorded on a disk. The first monograph serves to establish part of a treatise with plates, then a special encyclopedia (zoological), then a general encyclopedia. The works are cataloged in a library, after having been announced at publication (publisher catalogs and Bibliography of France). The documents are recopied (drawings, watercolors, paintings, statues, photos, films, microfilms), then selected, analyzed, described, translated (documentary productions). The documents that relate to this event are the object of a scientific classifying (fauna) and of an ideologic [idéologique] classifying (classification). Their ultimate conservation and utilization are determined by some general techniques and by methods that apply to all documents—methods that are studied in national associations and at international Congresses.

The cataloged antelope is an initial document and the other documents are secondary or derived. (Briet 2006, 9–11)[2]

In the above passage, Briet is arguing for a notion of the document as *indice* that is a critical expansion of a notion of document as *evidence*, by means of the addition of arguments by "linguists and philosophers" (i.e., at her time and place of writing, likely by practitioners of structural linguistics and semiotics). Documentary evidence takes place in networks of signs that encompass people and things, the explicitness of those networks being even more apparent to the general public in what she termed "secondary documents" (popular and professional discourses) rather than "initial documents" (e.g., taxonomies, indexes, ontologies, etc.). Indice *are socio-technical devices that have technological and social logics enfolded within them as meaningful functions for information organization and use and they give rise to and mediate the social positioning and information and knowledge values of texts and person as documents, information, and data.* Consequently they are also signs within, and which point to, the political economy of knowledge and being within which a text and its referents take place. They are important points that direct identity and action for human beings. *Indice* are signs that not only reference empirical and ideational entities, but signify by condensing and pointing toward actual and potential meaningful pasts, presents, and futures, along which human beings develop, understand, and live. They are entranceways and exits for desire and are representations of forms of life.

In her book, Briet (2006) formulated an example of a documentary sign, a newly discovered antelope and its being named as such within institutional and cultural structures. The animal becomes a named being by being placed or indexed within accepted regimes of documentary cultural forms and social norms. It becomes a type of animal, an antelope, upon its capture, housing in a zoo, and being named within taxonomic and institutional structures, and then in its circulation in popular and professional discourses.

For Briet this social life of a typologically named entity—that is, of a documented form—is very important. Documentation for Briet is a *cultural technique* (Briet 2006; Day 2006). It is a cultural technique in two senses: a technique of documentary management in specialized libraries and documentation centers, and a cultural technique in so far as documentation continues modernity through helping (and for Briet, leading, through documentary "prospecting") scientific investigations (Briet 2006). As we will see, one importance of this cultural informatics is that documents as *indice* constitute a nexus of representation that change texts and persons into information objects and users. *The documentary typology of individuals is a distinguishing characteristic of sociocultural modernity.*

According to Briet (2006), documentation is a "necessity of our time." Its necessity emerges from information overload in modernity and from the needs of scientists and engineers (as well as others) to have quick and efficient access to the newest information in their own and neighboring subject domains. For Briet, specialized cultures make up the culture of modernity, but the culture of modernity is overall driven by greater needs for "efficiency" and "dynamism," and this includes in intellectual domains. New techniques and technologies respond to these needs, but they also create a "new rhythm" of "intellectual work" (Briet 2006; Day 2006).

Conceptually, Briet's argument that documents are "cultural techniques" and her vindication of documentation as a leading "necessity" for scientific modernity suggests that the modern documentary tradition constitutes an important modern episteme that defines us both through our technical and everyday practices. This "new rhythm" of documentary modernity, which constitutes our lives via the mediation of information and communication technologies, is an important part of what *Indexing It All* traces and analyzes through its chosen cases. The book engages questions such as: What are the consequences of this rhythm of the modern documentary tradition and its different moments of development for psychological senses of self, others, and groups? What are the political consequences of this new rhythm and its episteme? How is knowledge and agency being reshaped? With Briet's notion of the *indice* in mind, this book creates a documentary variation of "social positioning theory" (a term used by the philosopher Rom Harré and various of his coauthors) to ask: How do we socially and culturally position ourselves and others by means of documentary technologies and techniques? What are the social and technical roles and rules that govern the positioning of ourselves as documentation, information, and data users and objects? Of course, no single answer can be given to such large questions, so this book attempts a set of readings of historical and conceptual cases and offers these cases and their readings as tools for the reader's consideration.

Indexing It All examines five cases in the next five chapters, followed by a concluding chapter that looks at the problem of the sites and time of critique. To help the reader get an overview of the book I have summarized some of the content of the chapters below.

Chapter 2: Paul Otlet: Friends and Books for Information Needs

This chapter is an extended exegesis upon two statements, one from the "father of European documentation," Paul Otlet, made in 1903 on the

topic of books (and more generally documents'
used friends, and the other from the philosop'
in 1938 on the topic of libraries. The chapte'
spectives on books, libraries, and friendship as ι.
and social shifts in the meaning of textuality and peι.
meneutic (Heidegger) to an instrumental (Otlet) basis. Chapι.
rest of the book's reading of a modern documentary tradition thaι.
the spirit of Otlet's sociotechnical instrumentalism.

Chapter 3: Representing Documents and Persons in Information Systems: Library and Information Science and Citation Indexing and Analysis

This chapter begins with a discussion of how the shift from documentation to information science was achieved in the discourse and practice of
the academic research field of library and information science in the late
twentieth century through a theoretical understanding of information and
information needs as concepts of "aboutness" or representation. This discussion includes analysis of key articles by the library and information science scholar Michael Buckland. The chapter examines the understanding
of persons and texts as capable of being represented in terms of information
or "aboutness," an understanding that transforms texts and persons into
being information and users (the latter characterized as having information
needs). This chapter then examines citation indexes as sociotechnical systems through which subjects become further transformed into documentary representation or "information."

Chapter 4: Social Computing and the Indexing of the Whole

Building on the previous discussions, in this chapter I investigate the further transformation of persons and texts into documentary representations
within broader-based indexing systems, namely social computing systems
through retrieval and social networking algorithms. The chapter looks at
persons and texts as being historically subsumed (Hegel and Marx's *Aufhebung*) within sociotechnical logics. In a discussion of Althusser's concepts of
ideology and interpellation, I compare them to the computational interpolation of data. The chapter then covers style and taste as some of the dominant social trends that are used to index documentary subjects and objects
together within indexes of information needs and their fulfillments.

er 5: The Document as the Subject: Androids

is chapter emphasizes not the documentary becoming of the subject, but rather the subjective becoming of the document, in attempts to build android robots through an affective and communicational dialectic with people. Whereas in the previous chapters I emphasized the subsumption of human agency within information systems, in this chapter I discuss the attempt to embody human agency within an information system that appears like a human being. Here the term "documents" refers to sets of codes that operate the android and to the meaningful interactions that appear through, and then remediate our further interactions with android machines.

Chapter 6: Governing Expression: Social Big Data and Neoliberalism

In this chapter I discuss the mutual reduction of documentary subjects and objects to being conjoined points of data within systems of social "big data." I examine big data as a technique of governance, particularly through neoliberal capitalism and the governments that serve it: subjects are tracked within "trends" that are functions of markets, while at the same time these markets and their trends make up the expressions of the properly cultured and socialized subject, increasingly understood as "innovative" or "trend-setting" agents within capital markets. Social big data indexing and analysis aim toward variable and parametric representations of subjects as such agents (or threats against capitalism) over time, and are put under surveillance through these. The chapter ends with a critical discussion of what Katherine Hayles (2012) calls "hyper" or "surface" reading, the skimming or surveillance of texts through documentary means in order to answer information needs. Hyper or surface reading can be understood as a mode of information literacy and of acts of reading accomplished by skimming.

Chapter 7: Conclusion: The Modern Documentary Tradition and the Site and Time of Critique

The conclusion poses the problem of the sites and time of critique when people and their rights of judgment are being increasingly mediated, displaced, and replaced by modern documentary techniques, technologies, and methods. Can there be critique in an age and society of what Suzanne Briet called "homo documentator," particularly when combined with the conditions and demands of neoliberal capitalism? What are the rights of beings in the midst of a society that so broadly measures being by documentary representation?

2 Paul Otlet: Friends and Books for Information Needs

To start our investigation in this chapter, I provide an exegesis on the relation of persons to documents through rather traditional documentary and institutional forms in modernity: books as documents and libraries as containers for documents. Starting from two fragments from the beginning of the twentieth century—a quote from the European documentalist Paul Otlet and a later quote from the philosopher Martin Heidegger—this chapter explicates two overlapping and competing traditions about the relationship between persons and texts. With Otlet's quote we begin to see the development of what would, toward the end of the twentieth century, be called the "information age." Texts become documents with information, and persons become users with information needs. These changes brought with them an increasingly instrumental and technological view toward knowledge, increasingly leaving behind and demoting an older hermeneutics of understanding. Significantly, in Otlet's text the instrumental and technological view toward knowledge and being occurs around the trope of books as friends.[1]

The book-friend metaphor that Otlet reinterprets is important for several reasons. First, because this is a very traditional trope in the Western cultural tradition, reaching back to ancient works. Second, because Otlet's reinterpretation overlaps with the important German nineteenth- and early twentieth-century hermeneutic tradition (represented by Dilthey, Heidegger, and later, Gadamer), where textual hermeneutics is read analogously with psychological (or in the case of Heidegger, ontological) hermeneutics. Third, the extension of this metaphor to libraries, understood as places of books, characterizes libraries as places where human interpretative understanding and self-understanding takes place—in other words, libraries become sites for understanding (and therefore friendship) between peoples (and for individuals understanding themselves, as well).

As we will see below, Paul Otlet, arguably the founder of European documentation, directly challenged the hermeneutic sense of the book-friend trope by characterizing texts as friends that are consulted as informational containers for answers to specific questions from their interrogators. For Otlet, these book (or more generally, document) "friends" and their answers are too numerous to count, but are technically organized and are consulted by what we now call the "user" for the purposes of the user's needs through libraries of documents and the techniques and technologies for information retrieval. In Otlet's works we begin to see the familiar language of documentation and library and information science in the later twentieth century in its characterization of documents as containers of information, which act as efficient and effective answers to user information needs.

Against Otlet's technologized vision of the document as an instrumental friend, we will posit Martin Heidegger's brief criticism of modern academic libraries as organizational forms within the instrumentalization of knowledge in modern academic and research systems. Heidegger's criticism is of academic research libraries as documentary warehouses within large, modern, institutional systems of knowledge production. In Heidegger's quote, such libraries are contrasted with personal libraries as personal spaces for human understanding—a literally more *intimate* relationship between books and persons. Heidegger ironically suggests that private libraries are no longer needed by scholars, now that scholarship has been inscribed within larger business relationships for research.

These are brief quotes, but the exegeses performed in this chapter are meant to read them as symptoms of larger historical problematics that will be engaged throughout the book. As I have suggested elsewhere (Day 2001), to take Otlet or Heidegger's positions on such questions as merely representing their opinion or even different disciplinary fields would be to radically reduce the social and political importance that both historical figures attributed to their works, and to reduce the importance that their works have achieved within intellectual history in the twentieth century. In both their works, such quotes are metonymic parts of wholes; they speak to their authors' positions regarding major issues of knowledge and being in modernity, positions that are reflected throughout each scholar's larger oeuvre. It is important to start this book by intensely focusing on this question of human relationships to texts and documents in order to work out in the other chapters the meanings of being and knowledge that occur later in the modern documentary tradition.

The modern problem of the book-friend and of the library-site brings issues of being and knowledge in documentary modernity into focus. While the Otlet and Heidegger quotes that I will present are separated by twenty-five years and are now roughly a century old, they still represent competing claims for knowledge and being that are being worked out today, not only in the forms of paper documents and libraries, but throughout our everyday lives via online digital documents and computer mediation in their access and retrieval. The consequences of this evolution shape our universities, our texts, our visions of science and knowledge, our relationships to our past and to other cultures, and our relationships to one another. Today, we are witnessing the dominance of the modern documentary tradition that Otlet championed and the waning of Heidegger's hermeneutic and philosophical tradition, and this evolution has its good and bad consequences that need to be considered.

Paul Otlet and the Informational Friend

We will start with the quote from the beginning of the twentieth century, from the European documentalist Paul Otlet. As a Comtean positivist in the context of the cultural politics of aesthetic form that were widespread in Europe in the early part of the twentieth century—ranging from Soviet revolutionary art on the one hand to fascist aesthetics on the other—Otlet's material commitments regarding documents have explicit epistemic and political ramifications. His understanding of documents as *in-forme* (content that fills or "in-forms") contested earlier understandings of knowledge and its material forms, and it attempted to enact a politics of systemic knowledge use and progress based on the mediating power of information and communication techniques and technologies.

Otlet's 1903 quote was published as part of an article in the *Bulletin* of the International Institute of Bibliography (number 8), which would later become the International Federation for Information and Documentation, founded by Otlet and his colleague Henri La Fontaine (see Rayward 1994). The article's title, "Les sciences des bibliographiques et la documentation," is translated by W. Boyd Rayward as "The Science of Bibliography and Documentation." Otlet writes,

Today, there exist collections of books comprising more than two million volumes and whose annual accessions are more than one hundred thousand volumes. They have had to come to grips with quite new problems arising, on the one hand, from difficulties of storage, classification and circulation of such tremendous masses of materials situated in the centres of large cities, and on the other hand, from new ideas within the research community about what it should be able to gain from such resources. Once, one read; today one refers to, checks through, skims. *Vita brevis ars longa!* There is too much to read; the times are wrong; the trend is no longer slavishly to follow the author through the maze of a personal plan which he has outlined for himself and which, in vain, he attempts to impose on those who read him.

Works are referred to, that is to say, one turns to them to ask for a reply to very precise, specialized questions. The reply found, one parts company, ungratefully no doubt but certainly for a thousand good reasons, from the obliging friend who has just given such good service. It rarely happens that an adequate reply is found in a single book and that it is not necessary to obtain such a reply from a combination of partial answers provided by a variety of works. Thus arises the necessity of having available great quantities of works, as many as possible; thus, also, the obligation of not systematically eliminating any work from book collections because little importance or value is attributed to it. Who can make a pronouncement on the usefulness or uselessness of a document when so many interpretations of the same text are possible, when so many former truths are recognized as wrong today, when so many accepted facts have been modified by more recent discoveries; when, in the present anarchy of intellectual production, so few questions have been dealt with exhaustively by a single author; and when, so often, it is necessary to be content with a half-truth or run the risk of remaining in a state of complete ignorance?

The number of works which libraries contain increases the need for documentation, just as organs develop functions. This need, in its turn, acts strongly on the necessary enlargement of collections of books. But this process cannot be confined to the realm of large libraries. It spreads beyond them through the diffusion of the works themselves. More reliable, better arranged, more up-to-date books can be produced because of the improved bibliographical apparatus of these libraries. Such books become models that, naturally, intellectual workers, who otherwise only have access to inferior bibliographical equipment, wish to imitate and surpass. Such books lead us to pose very clearly the problem of documentation in relation to libraries of the second rank. (Otlet 1990, 79–80)

The article from which this quote is taken begins with the rather peculiar, but traditionally recognizable, trope of speaking about books as if they were persons—friends, to be exact. The article proceeds as a sort of science or physiology of the book as a mentally enlarged person by additional information, a knowledge economy that in later works Otlet many times traced in his notion of an ecological system of knowledge, in which books play the metonymical role of being both a material object and a generalized documentary concept, and always a supplement to the human brain, both of an author and collectively of civilization.

This emblematic passage is interesting for several reasons. First, it starts with the problem of what has been termed "information overload." Since the late nineteenth century it has been claimed that information overload has brought about the need for new information management and retrieval technologies. As Suzanne Briet (2006) put it, these technologies then respond and introduce a "new rhythm" to our lives. Otlet's documentary concept of the book-friend is, thus, part of this new rhythm imposed by the "necessity" of new information management and retrieval technologies. Where before we could dwell in the author's book, now we search it/him for information. "*Vita brevis ars longa!*"—we simply don't have the time to dwell on the book or friend as a whole and for his own sake. We look for what we need, which corresponds to something already known in some primitive form, at least (e.g., a term). The informational book is, thus, a document: it provides information on something we know something about, at least enough to want to know more about it. In other words, we are looking for, in the sense of the modern documentary tradition, "evidence"—evidence for some question or need that we, the user, has. Second, the passage suggests a determined and striking instance of not simply a documentary, but a *sociological* and a *psychological* shift in Western culture. The traditional trope of books as friends, which understands both books and friends as texts for companionship, communication, knowledge, and self-knowledge, now shifts in Otlet's view to understanding books and friends as information containers that satisfy specific questions—information needs ("One turns to them to ask for a reply to very precise, specialized, questions"). Last, for Otlet a single book is seen as inadequate for answering a question. A question worth asking demands many replies, which demands many books (and other documentary types), and so the bibliographical or documentary universe for satisfying a reader vastly expands beyond a single document into networks of documents.

Within Otlet's notion of the book-document as a response to user inquiries, our digital present age is foreseen, with its fading traditional book and traditional libraries in a universe of quickly expanding networks of digital forms and documentary types, most assuming small documentary sizes and communicational forms. For Otlet, smaller chunks of texts, taken from larger texts, could be arranged on cards or on sheets according to his "monographic principle" (Rayward 1994), whereby the essential "facts" of a document themselves constituted a document. For Otlet, the universal book (*Livre universel*) was a general trope for all sorts of documentary types

(Otlet 1934). For Otlet, the notion of "the book" referred to both particular books and what he took to be the universal book, which is a synonym for all documentary types and information.

Both Otlet's utilitarian fragmentation of books and his concept of the universal book resemble the generalization and dissolution of the notion of "friends" in our day. There may still be "best friends" for children and adolescents, but many young people in modern countries are members of computationally mediated social networks and have hundreds or thousands of online friends. The notion of "friend" now is both fragmented and generic, particularly in regard to documentary texts. What once may have been a metaphor is now a social fact: the (digital) friend is no longer *like* a text in terms of his or her complexity of inscriptional weavings that require reading. He or she *is* a document, mediated through the availability and computational processing of documentary fragments that correspond to a user's needs.

Social media is made up of evidentiary fragments that say: *this is what I am (about)*. In modernity, documentary aboutness gives identity. The document represents the person as a symbolic image of being. The document is not a *textus* or a weaving whose beginnings and ends are hard to discern. Nor does signification appear and then retreat in the phenomenon of friendship and reading the friend's actions. The documentary chunks of texts, like the characteristics and expressions of people, are viewed as optimally being distinct and quantifiable—"clear writing" or "clear expression" as is said in the Anglo-American cultural tradition. One seeks one's friends as information for one's needs and one deploys a self for the same purposes within a general economy or market of need-based representations.

Our reading of the reversibility of the metaphor of books and friends in Otlet's work is not just retrospective. It is justified not only by the 1903 article, but also by the entire context of Otlet's work in documentation and world standardization (currency, universities, and so on). For Otlet, the social and the documentary had a direct mapping onto each other, the latter serving toward mutual understanding and the advancement of knowledge. Otlet's work was dedicated to world peace, arguing for the reorganization of documents, cultures, and societies through larger, international, structures. Otlet's vision of bibliography foresaw distance information delivery for users via the delivery of printed text across television screens (Otlet 1935). But Otlet's politics remained largely grounded in a vision of the world governed by elites like him. As limited as this vision was for democratic participation, Otlet's understanding of documentation and its information argued for the fusion of social space, knowledge forms, and information and communication technologies in creating a "world brain."

Otlet's quote proposes an instrumental shift in the understanding of documents and people, of which today we are only beginning to feel the full effects.

Martin Heidegger: The Value of Libraries

We will now turn to our second quote, this by the famous German philosopher Martin Heidegger, whose approach was hermeneutic phenomenology. The quote is found within a public lecture of 1938, translated into English as "The Age of the World Picture" (Heidegger 1977a). In this lecture, Heidegger continues his critique of political and social modernity as reductive systems upon beings and the question of being. For Heidegger, mass psychology and the mass media aid this reduction by valorizing and reifying the discourses and norms of knowledge that are communicated in what he called in his earlier book, *Being and Time*, an "everyday" (*Alltäglichkeit*) manner (Heidegger 1962). The lecture ends by presenting the history of metaphysics in the West as a history of the increasing power and social breadth of instrumental and reductive *techne*, developing into modern technologies and culminating in the sociotechnical governance systems of Soviet communism and American commercialism. For Heidegger, both of these political economies turn away from an ontologically authentic encounter with the human manner of engaging being, namely in terms of the experience of time as finitude, which human *Dasein* (existence) experiences in its being-with (*Mitsein*) others. From an experience of finitude born out of the awareness of death through others, *Dasein* shows care and solicitude toward others, and drifts in and out of moods that are based on the attunement of *Dasein* to other beings (Heidegger 1962). All these attributes, for Heidegger, follow from an ontological, rather than an ontic mode of existence; they are philosophically accessible through a fundamental phenomenological ontology, rather that through a psychological analysis, which in the Western tradition privileges the subject and his or her will (Heidegger 1962).

In thinking through textuality and friendship in Heidegger's work, it is necessary to recall this priority of an ontological or fundamental way of being over the ontic or "everyday being" of *Dasein*. The primacy of *Mitsein* comes to define for Heidegger both our way of being with other people, and in his later work—shaded by an overarching concern with language that even goes beyond that concern in *Being and Time*—something like *Mitsein* inhabits our way of being with texts, as well. With both friends and texts, we dwell within language as what Heidegger often called the "the house of being," and from this dwelling we gain both the possibilities of understanding and misunderstanding both others and ourselves. Otlet was concerned with the textual or psychological other as a source of information for the subject's needs (founded upon the assumption that language is a conduit through which information is to be transmitted); in contrast, for Heidegger language is not a conduit for information, but rather it is what binds both the reader and the text, as well as friends, together in the possibility of being understood. Language thus first of all reveals being—with informational correctness or incorrectness, usefulness or non-usefulness occurring in subsequent modes of functioning only through the prior affordances of an already shared language.

In Otlet's works, documentary forms are for information exchange (i.e., they are for communication through a text). Information exchange according to this model involves the transmission of representations from one mind to another; what M. J. Reddy (1979) termed the "conduit metaphor," which was a widely enough available trope for understanding the general function of language at the beginning of the twentieth century that it started off Saussure's lectures in general linguistics from 1906 to 1911 (Saussure 2011). In contrast, for Heidegger, *communication* is grounded in an ontological mode of being, *Mitsein*; a foundational relationship of *community* within which discourses and understanding may exist. The erasure of this ontology in the ontic reading of *Dasein* (as subjectivity) and *Mitsein* (as dialectics and broadly understood exchange values for informational and communicative representations) constitutes for Heidegger one of the culminating signs of Western metaphysics. In short, Heidegger's project of the *Destruktion* of Western metaphysics (Heidegger 1962) (influencing, later, Derrida's deconstruction of Western metaphysics) is precisely the destruction of the metaphysics of presence that characterizes Otlet's notion of "information" and the modern documentary tradition's notion of documents, information, and data as self-evident evidence.

With this general background in mind, let us at last turn to the Heidegger passage. It is brief, but it occupies a notable place within Heidegger's text, "The Age of the World Picture" (Heidegger 1977a), which began as a public lecture on June 9, 1938, on the topic of the role of metaphysics in producing the image of the modern world. Heidegger's characterization of the modern university in his lecture foreshadowed the even greater character of the modern research university under the umbrella of "big science" in the period after World War II, particularly in the United States, but also in Europe. For Heidegger, modern science is characterized by theoretical framings and methodological processes carried out by technical and technological devices under the guidance of methods, which result in objective statements about things and events that are studied in the natural sciences and about subjects and their behaviors in the social sciences. Humanities scholarship, however, doesn't know this distance. Its texts are not documents, in Otlet's sense of being statements of "object-ive" truth about things and events.

Heidegger writes:

The research man no longer needs a library at home. Moreover, he is constantly on the move. He negotiates at meetings and collects information at congresses. He contracts for commissions with publishers. The latter now determine along with him which books must be written. (Heidegger 1977a, 125)

The proximity of a personal library where books can be marked up, that is, dialogued with and critically interrogated, is important for Heidegger because a book, like other textual forms, is an interweaving of signification that the reader disentangles and interprets. This engagement with the text is so important because it is an occasion for an event of understanding and self-understanding in the transformation of both the meaning of the text (via reading) and of the person reading it. This is the basis for the tradition of hermeneutics as reading and understanding—a tradition that runs from medieval biblical hermeneutics through historical and social science hermeneutics of the nineteenth and twentieth centuries (Gadamer 2004). Heidegger's quote contrasts hermeneutically driven scholarship with modern scientific research as representation through different notions of the library. Although textual composition makes up a large part of what is considered to be science or not, scientific texts largely follow methods of rhetorical composition that frame the text as a *reporting* and a *representation* of something outside of the text, implying that textual composition is a secondary event in the scientific process and in the establishment of scientific truth. This very rhetorical framing often gives to new or previously unscientific fields of research, as well as established ones, the value and truth claims of being "science."

For Heidegger (1977a), in the modern research university, texts are treated as documents containing information, which are then usefully appropriated with other documents and information toward advancing research. The academic circulation of documents and information is often guided by research projects that follow grants and publishing opportunities. Libraries or other information sources are viewed as part of this apparatus of production and reproduction. The needs of the scholarly user thus are often defined or refined by the system of scientific production in which they are located. As Otlet wrote, documents are consulted as to what a reader needs, rather than as a site for the fusion of hermeneutic horizons between reader and writer via an exploration of language and thought through the semantic interweavings of the language of the text.

In the quote above, Heidegger is describing an element in not only what later would be called "big science," but also the modern technocratic university that is part of such, where the scholar's work is driven by research agendas, publishing opportunities, and research funding sources that are established by "science," understood as the dominant political economy and business of knowledge. "Science," in this sense, is understood as formally or informally collaborative and systemic research procedures and authorship, privately and publically funded, which are project based and epistemically grounded in empirically generated "information," whose current privileged form in our day is now quantifiable "data." The contrast between science and humanities scholarship, when it does exist today, at least in terms of hermeneutics, is between documents as containers of information, which are consulted for the information that they representationally contain, and texts, understood through close readings and a type of understanding that involves both a bridging of hermeneutic horizons and a critical and sometimes formally performative questioning of their topics by the style of these very texts.

Smaller libraries could support the epistemic tradition that Heidegger was working from, namely, that of Western philosophy in the continental vein. In the medieval university, where books were hard to come by as compared to the modern period, students and scholars were expected to know and repeat the arguments surrounding philosophical issues. In Heidegger's era and still today in some corners, philosophy relied and relies upon a relatively small historical canon of authors and their texts, viewed as exemplary lenses into historical traditions of concepts.

The expansion of research into the function and definition of academic libraries during the twentieth century and especially after World War II has radically challenged the hermeneutic model of science and scholarship. More recently, the availability of online bibliographies and full-text retrieval since the 1990s has made primary and secondary texts widely available in every field, increasing the amount and importance of documentary evidence in scholarly writing, both at the professional and the student level. And at the level of undergraduate education, composition classes in the American university for the past thirty or so years have emphasized demonstrative composition using cited documents as evidence, rather than argumentative rhetoric using cited texts for close reading and exegesis.

Heidegger's argument about the nature of libraries in the above quote takes place in the context of an emerging quantitative research agenda in the social sciences and its use by the Nazi, Soviet, and the American corporatist state. However, the vision of the library as a place of information and data storage and retrieval, a place supporting direct or indirect economic production more fully than only scholarly research, would come during the twentieth century to inscribe almost every type of library.

Information Infrastructures and Time

In the Otlet and Heidegger quotes above, books and libraries are both literal and metonymical tokens for larger social and cultural contestations regarding the nature of knowledge and its social origins and roles. Indeed, the entire problematic of the local and the familiar in Heidegger's later works may be read as having begun with a concern with the problem of time in modernity, which occupied his first major book, *Being and Time*, and which subsequently in his later works becomes more explicitly political and explicitly pointed as a critique of modern technology as Western metaphysics. Heidegger's concern for libraries and publishing systems as sites for thinking are no less concerned with this problematic of time. In parallel, the issue for us here is that of the text as a site for the unfolding of time as a human event of understanding and the document as a tool within productionist systems—and consequently to this—the issue of information infrastructures and the construction of time that occurs through them in relation to being and political economy.

As has been mentioned, Suzanne Briet noted the significant role that information and communication devices have in constructing the "rhythms" of human life in modernity, particularly as they increase efficiency. For Briet, documentation serves a forward and progressive notion of time, characterized by efficiency in the fulfillment of tasks and needs, which often takes the tropic form in Briet's work of "science." This modern notion of progressive time and efficient temporality is folded into twentieth-century documentality both in theory (i.e., in the social justification of documentation) and in the design and use of technical systems, respectively. The "coolness" of today's images of the young urban professional or the busy mother multitasking with mobile devices is just one recent example. As Geof Bowker (2005) has shown in his research on geological epistemology and classification in the nineteenth century, documentary systems and empirical temporal forms may be enfolded in very explicit manners, with evidence of geological time through geological layering read according to the very archival arrangements of the records and the records read according to geological notions of layering. (A like example is found in Freud's documentary notions of the mind, understood along lines of a geological dig, which is then read as an archive.) As Otlet's quote makes clear, quickness and efficiency of information transfer are central concerns for him in the use of books and other documentary forms. For Otlet, reading is information transfer, which depends upon information storage and retrieval.

As with all information retrieval systems (as compared with paper document or physical shelf browsing), one has to know or be prompted with the vocabulary of what one is looking for in advance of getting the information. Thus, an "information need" within information retrieval requires a pre-understanding which coordinates future understandings that are developed from it. Central for Otlet was the problem of how to organize a library or other information infrastructure as collections and as retrieval devices in order to serve information needs. For this, Otlet and Henri LaFontaine invented, based on the Dewey Decimal Classification (DDC) system, the Universal Decimal Classification (UDC) system. Otlet also organized l'Institut international de bibliographie, he founded the Mundaneum in

Brussels (which housed a massive world library), and he engaged in many other such projects, such as planning a world bank, a world university, and a world city (Rayward 1975). Both Otlet's technical and organizational structures acted as, broadly understood, pre-coordinate indexes for the materials that they held or for materials that they referred to outside of their domains and institutions.

What, essentially, are modern indexes? Modern indexes are lists of vocabulary that indicate their referents in ways that most expedite the finding and retrieval of those referents. Indexes must refer to items in the most *precise* means possible. (Precision is characterized by the correspondence of recall to need, but in fact, since need can often not be articulated before search, assumptions of precision help define need in recursive movements of a search.)

Pre-coordinate indexes are the largely explicit and "transcendental" vocabularies and their organization that are the technical means for retrieval within classical documentary systems. With computational post-coordinate systems, where the user forms the search by user-input search terms (either originating from the user's natural language or combined from controlled vocabulary), some algorithms can mimic the precision of pre-coordinate indexing through statistical inference from records (or social or physical relationships) and build indexes and retrieval ranking in that manner. In modern computational algorithms the techniques of post-coordinate indexing tend to be more "hidden" and infrastructural for the user.

Both pre- and post-coordinate indexes and their logics or algorithms of construction are created and implemented in order to facilitate ease and efficiency in information seeking and retrieval. Akin to other modern techniques and technologies, it may be said that indexes reduce the "transaction costs" (in human time and effort) of searching. The trade-off is that the searches are often done through abbreviated representations or fragments of documentary materials, which constitute the indexes through which search is done. As we will later discuss, social computing software enfold normative psychological assumptions and behavioral practices within their algorithms.

Information infrastructures lower transaction costs, and they do so with increasing transparency in their use as they become more ubiquitous and nontransparent in their construction and even presence. One could make this argument for any modern technical or technological infrastructure, however. Transportation systems lower the transaction costs of movement and effort. Sewers and clean water, and pollution control more generally, lower the transaction costs imposed by poor health, for individuals and society as a whole. One can view the notion of "transaction cost" financially of course, but perhaps the more important sense is when it is taken as a generalized statement regarding expenditure, namely, human energy expenditure, which in modernity is often factored as time.

The other side of this, though, and from a Heideggerian perspective a much darker philosophical and social side, is that modern social infrastructures generally, and modern information infrastructures more particularly, take a general economy of interaction and mediate it through more restrictive economies of production. The lowering of transaction costs depends upon increasing efficiency, and increasing efficiency depends on repetitive systemic and behavioral operations. Expressions are recycled back into the technological-human system in order to improve efficiency and further lower transaction costs. Human experiential time is recalculated as systems notions of time, resulting in concepts of "wasting" or "saving" time, often based on various types of expenditure and profit models and metaphors.

The need for modern infrastructure development has occurred because of several demands: Increased population in modern cities (which themselves are modern infrastructures for reducing transaction costs of travel and communication over distances) has resulted in the need for sewers, water supply, and electrical transmission. Increased distances between people have resulted in transportation infrastructures (which themselves can add to the distances traveled, as we have seen in the case with the growth of suburbs after World War II). Nationalization and internationalization require regulation and standardization for transactions, commercial ports, record keeping, documents, and officiating bureaucracies for mediating different standards. Finally, the mixing of national and ethnic peoples in modernity requires accessible universal language signs, translation skills, and technologies for facilitating communication and understanding, and also requires notions of fundamental human rights that are legally and ethically respected and enforced.

Information infrastructures, as Bowker (2005) has argued, come to shape what is understood as information or knowledge. Knowledge is shaped by infrastructures in two senses: as the "content" of texts and as the potential for action by individuals and groups. Lai Ma (Ma 2012) has suggested that information infrastructures, such as library classification and cataloging systems, have shaped documentation and information types and their theorization, as well, in the field of library and information science. Neal Thomas (2011) has shown how social computing algorithms, such as Google PageRank, play a central role in shaping knowledge by organizing social space and personal identity through algorithms that, for example, privilege popular personal or social choices and so shape the present nature and future possibilities of information and knowledge and of communicative choices.

Whether it be through pre-coordinate systems of classes and professionally authorized and organized terms or through post-coordinate inputs mediated by algorithms whose assumptions are either acknowledged or not, information infrastructures both reveal and hide pasts, presents, and the futures of objects and subjects, shaping both the form, and resultantly, the "content" of knowledge and information. Such infrastructures are, in the language of Derrida, Foucault, and others of the French poststructuralist era, *archae*-ological features of sociotechnical rationality.

Information infrastructures act indexically. They do so in several ways: they work upon and produce reduced formulations of vocabulary from texts and discourses; they collect, reflect, and deploy cultural forms and social norms in assumptions and practices toward "usefully" serving the users that use them; and they are often unseen or unacknowledged points of presence that join together past, present, and future meaning and value into webs of stable and useful reference. Information infrastructures contain indexes, in a restricted sense of this latter term, but they *are* indexes in a more general use of the term; they point to things, and they select, condense, and redeploy their documentary referents through manipulating fragments or representations of these. Importantly, they serve as social, cultural, and historical entranceways and exits not just for the things that they represent and mediate, but also, like all infrastructures for human agency and expression, by providing the means by which intentions may be expressed in meaningful expressions and actions and by which social hierarchies and orders are formed and reproduced. They provide the means for cultural, social, and physical affordances, increasingly not only through transparent manners or even non-transparent manners of symbol manipulation by machines, but also through using the very fact of one's physical existence as 'input parameters' for increasing or decreasing commercial and state governance and personal powers.

The protests in Heidegger's later writings against modern technology are precisely in terms of what he saw as modernity's appropriation of more general economies of human ways of being into increasingly restrictive economies of production as mediated by techniques and technologies. For Heidegger, these techniques and technologies decrease what we are calling "transaction costs," but they do so by restricting, marginalizing, and historically eliminating modes of human interaction and knowledge that are more "expensive" in terms of time and understanding.

Thus friendship, in the sense that Heidegger saw it (one may recall here that Heidegger's first book, *Being and Time*, was dedicated to his teacher Edmund Husserl "in friendship and admiration") could be read in terms of a general relationship of care and solicitude. In *Being and Time* friendship is understood in terms of relationships to other human beings through ontologically "primordial" forms of solicitude and care based on common modes of being, particularly as human beings experience their time and finitude as a constant concern. In contrast, the durational speeding up of understanding and of knowledge (of both people and texts) characterizes the modern sense of technological being, whereby human beings as *Dasein* find themselves cast out of what Heidegger analyzed in *Being and Time* as more ontologically "authentic" modes of being into ontic modes (Heidegger 1962). Such ontic modes of being are often then conceptually reified and methodologically quantified in social science research and by computational algorithms. Such modern beings experience time not as a quality of their fundamental mode of existence or as their common belonging within living (particularly human) beings, but time as a quality of modernity's technological productivity. By 1964, in his lecture "The End of Philosophy and the Task of Thinking" (Heidegger 1977b), this mode of understanding and knowledge is seen by Heidegger to extend even to art expressions, which according to Heidegger are understood in terms of a cybernetic economy of communication, wherein art is said to *transmit information*—that is to say, transmit the ideas that the works are said to be about or contain.

In Heidegger's phenomenological analysis in *Being and Time*, "fuzzy" psychological phenomena such as moods play a central role in one's "attunement" to other people and to the world at large. This attunement or tonality (*Stimmung*) comes from hearing (*Hören*), rather than simply listening to and communicating with others. Foremost of importance is that of hearing the alterity or radical otherness of others, to which one is most attuned by one's very being in common with them. Heidegger argues that moods and other such attunements constitute more ontologically "primordial" or authentic comportments toward self and others than the cognitive or emotional ontic states that are privileged in modern psychological theory—not the least in regard to an experience of time, since for Heidegger such attunements are constituted primarily with the appearance of human senses of time and finitude in the moods of boredom, concern, anxiety, and so forth. Moods are not "states" that the subject *has*, but rather, phenomena that *have* both the subjects and what they are attending to. For Heidegger, these moods, which modern psychology takes as simply other emotional states, show relations of persons to themselves and to one another in terms of human experiences of time. Ontologically speaking, one doesn't *have* time either to save or to waste; one is held within the experience of time, as an experience of concern or solicitude toward one's self and others. Moods, which come and go upon us, show us as products of such concern, fundamentally belonging within the temporality of human being.

In contrast to this understanding of moods as shifting and temporally varying relationship to others and one's own being, there has been an increasing attempt in modern information systems to measure moods, from the questionnaires of twentieth-century American quantitative sociology and opinion surveys to more contemporary attempts to measure moods through the collection and analysis of social big data, and correlating such with economic and other indexes (see for example: Bollen, Goncalves, Ruan, and Mao 2011; Bollen, Mao, and Zeng 2011). Such an appropriation of moods follows the evaluation of attention, leisure, work, and many other aspects of human life by quantitative measures, indexes, and algorithms, often for linking such events to economic and financial metrics. The goal is, of course, to transform *Dasein*'s solicitude, its modes of being-concerned and the moods that are part of this, and its being as *Mitsein*, to social systems and economic measures of "productivity" (and consumption, in so far as this is seen as contributing to productivity), ultimately resulting in financial extractions of profit from ontological "surplus value." Moods and other such events are quantified according to behavioral markers and calculated and predicted over time.

For Heidegger, such indexes have the effect of funneling our ontologically authentic modes of being into ontic productionist drives, following what we could call "ideological" paths for expression. Modern psychological measurement and their indexes for Heidegger provide the illusion of a way of quantitatively grasping the indefiniteness of moods that take hold of us, explaining our psychological being in terms of economies of individual-agent causes and effects that can be represented, predicted, and psychologically corrected. They seek to provide a way to manage such moods by manipulating events that might affect such moods and to condition such moods toward cognitive decision making. (The inescapability of these ontological qualities, however, is insisted upon by our inability to remain outside of them: we become anxious to do the next thing and so become anxious about ourselves; we work and become bored; we constantly get drawn into concerns for others even in cases where our training as medical, legal, or other types of professionals demand that we keep clients, patients, and so forth at an "objective" distance; and foremost, we cannot escape for long thinking about ourselves and our actions in terms of our finitude and our relations toward one another, in a manner that is not restricted to instrumental relations.)

Heidegger's insistence upon mood and other "primordial" relationships raises the question of the modern sense of "information," "communication," and "knowledge": do these terms signify the transmission of meaning from an outside source (another person, for example) to a given subject, or do they signify an affect which both the subject and the other are within and are both expressing and expressed through? Correspondingly, understanding a library and reading as a place for, and an activity of, solicitude and reflection, versus simply being a site and an activity for busyness and production and information transfer at the service of user information needs, raises fundamental questions about being and knowledge in modernity.

Writing, Reading, Library

There is an ethics to the tropes of books as friends and of libraries as the place of these friends. The ethical questions occur in the rhetorical and social deployments of these tropes, which today must foremost be heard in the problem of the production of documents and data from texts, and of users and data from persons, and through the ability of information, communication, and knowledge systems to create and fulfill information, communication, and knowledge needs. The critical issue, then, is to be able to think about such needs socially, culturally, and physically, in terms of social, cultural, and institutional norms and affordances. "Needs" do not refer to personal needs alone, but to social and cultural needs, within which persons find what they think they are looking for. *The shift of the concepts of texts and libraries from being sites for self-reflection and the acquisition of knowledge to being sites for social and cultural consumption and production constitutes a major and important moment in the history of information, communication, and knowledge.*

If we follow Heidegger in his general critique of modern technology as the expression of the metaphysics of subjectivity and will, then we will see that driving this historical shift is an epistemology of documentation—and now, "information"—as the expression of metaphysics. This expression works through the technological mastery of otherness as sources for information, knowledge, and an idealized rational communication. Central to this *Geist* of modern metaphysics are indexes and the concept of the *indice* as mediators and symbols of the creation of subjects and objects of knowledge and expression, and the speeding up of the dialectic of informational subjects and objects in their correspondence and identity with each other. The metaphysics of the will to power is achieved technologically and technically, not just through the formalization and the production of documents, per se, but through the formalization and production of enunciations more generally *as documents*—that is, as documentary evidence or "information." In Marxist political theory, the formalization and production of enunciations was given the term "ideology," but that term seems so broad that some avoid using it today, as it may suggest being overtly political. But modern politics, most generally, is the relationship between actions and organized—in language, in society, and in institutions—wills to power. Indexes consolidate and give technical power to ideology, and ideology shapes the characteristics and forms of indexes. *Ideology and information techniques and technologies constitute the two poles of the dialectic of modern documentary indexicality.*

The tropes of books as friends and the library as the place of these friends, then, refer to political economies for human and textual identities, shaped by technological and cultural mediations of "needs to be informed," or simply put, "needs to know." Indexes constitute prisms for seeing and fulfilling these needs, giving them shape, and for changing moods and desires into specific information needs and their fulfillments. Indexes change the "fuzziness" of reading encounters into task-based learning systems.

As Suzanne Briet (2006) suggested, documentary modernity is shaped by the "rhythms" of its technologies, but these technologies are, too, shaped by the rhythms of social needs. Documentary or information needs take place in larger political economies than simply the subject's own desires, since those desires are socially constructed, both in a larger, epistemic sense and in the sense of pragmatics when we seek to find x information out of a field of information choices. Our "friendship" and our "dwelling" with texts are not results of empirical choices made by timeless and placeless agents of subjective free will (though, too, we also are not simply subjects of ideological systems).

In the next chapter I will explore the further documentary transformation of persons and texts through the historical transition from documentation to information (especially in the context of library and information science) and by examining citation indexing and analysis.

3   Representing Documents and Persons in Information Systems: Library and Information Science and Citation Indexing and Analysis

In this chapter, I examine the construction of subjective and objective identities and value within scholarly citation indexing and analysis, as an important historical and theoretical transition point between early twentieth-century documentation and later social computing. In such epistemic and historical transitions documentation and its practices are not left behind, but rather, they are gathered up in new techniques and technologies. These "moments" of the documentary episteme thus constitute their own "sub-epistemes," overlapping with each other in time and space, even as the dominance of certain techniques and technologies shift via progress in the precision and efficiency of need definition and fulfillment. Historically, one sees that the cognitive and the social distances between indexes and information needs that existed in a documentation tradition governed by structural pre-coordinate indexing and classification gradually becomes narrower in eras of large-scale, heterogeneous, "information" networks that are composed of broader economies of language and users and of infrastructural, post-coordinate and natural language, searching, and indexing. I start this chapter by discussing how documents became information in the field of library and information science, which is a small, but specific and useful discipline for understanding this transition within a modern documentary tradition.

As we will examine in this and the following chapter, historically and epistemically we are moving from the classificatory and naming functions of documentary structures to the assignment of personal and documentary identity as a *function* and a *product* of sociotechnical systems. Today, we are transitioning from a strictly documentary-informational episteme to a computer-mediated communicational one, though one that builds indexes and coordinates the construction of selves and persons by documentary-informational means. For better or worse, the ancient technological means that gave birth to "deep" thought are broadly giving way in scholarship and sociality to "surface" thought, dominated by social documentary mediation and communication networks. Even Western philosophical practice, for example, as an exemplar of the first, today seems to be increasingly positioned within situations of group practices and explicit institutional and socially mediated understandings, and less in single-authored canonical readings as compared to the distant and recent past. Given the ease at which human beings revert from documentary writing to oral communication, it is not hard to see that "deep" thinking has been a product of documentary and social structures (reaching back to ancient times, but particularly bourgeois social and documentary structures from the late eighteenth century on—i.e., books and their readers) that attempted to bridge distances and time through monographic documents, and that this technology appears in some ways to have been supplanted once again by a return to oral communication and newer written surrogates of such. Humans are social animals, and their success has largely been attributed to this characteristic via their advanced representational and communication skills, so it should be no surprise to see the epoch of documentation—indeed, even reaching back to ancient times—to be an historical "accident" born from, in some senses limited, technological affordances (as Plato seemed to say about writing in his *Phaedrus*) that served human social and environmental needs. Historically, the shift from older documentation to "new media" may be seen through these lenses, though documentary techniques remain central for organizing the new communication media as information producers and products, as well.

From Documents to Information

Mark Balnaves and Michele Willson in their book, *A New Theory of Information and the Internet* (2011) argue that there are two types of information retrieval traditions in modernity, what they call the "Cutter" and the "Otlet" traditions, after the works of the nineteenth-century classification theorist Charles Ammi Cutter, and that of Paul Otlet, the early twentieth-century founder of European documentation whose work was discussed in the previous chapter. For Balnaves and Willson, in the Cutter tradition the concept of information is taken as synonymous with the concept of documents in information retrieval, namely, as referring to containers for knowledge. To retrieve "information" is to retrieve a document (or surrogate of such in a bibliographical record, classification code, etc.). In contrast, what Balnaves and Willson call the Otlet tradition views information as a response to an information need (which is sometimes seen as a cognitive deficit)—in other words, as the product of the "transferal" of knowledge from the document to the user. Balnaves and Willson seem to see the first tradition as firmly rooted in the documentary and library traditions and the latter extending from information science out to cognitive science. As I argued in the previous chapter, indexes in the Otlet tradition have more than simply a retrieval function; they not only act as affordances and means for the fulfillment of "information needs," but for the creation of such, and the creation of documentary-mediated persons and selves, as well.

Balnaves and Willson's account is interesting and insightful, but particularly from the perspective of the discipline of library and information science (LIS), some may take it as an incomplete account.[1,2]

Those in the field of LIS, whose genealogy is very much made up of this documentary-information tradition, would immediately insert into Balnaves and Willson's account, for example, the name of Nicholas Belkin and his ASK (anomalous states of knowledge) model, which is usually associated with a "cognitive turn" in LIS and with much of the subsequent user studies and information-seeking behavior research that has been voluminous in LIS for the past thirty years or so. In Belkin's ASK model, the subject or "user" is seen as having "anomalous" states of knowledge that produce the information need, and the fulfilling of that need is said to result in a less cognitively "anomalous" state for the user. (In this aspect, ASK is a model of cognitive dissonance.) With ASK information needs are seen as products of individual cognitive lacks in two senses: in regard to the user's needs for becoming informed from documents or other information sources, and in regard to what the user may not be aware of in formulating a search. (This latter marks ASK's claims of being an advance over document-retrieval theory, as often associated with the Cranfield experiments of the 1960s on improving retrieval through improved indexing.)

The language of some of Belkin's theoretical formulations regarding ASK (e.g., Belkin,1977), namely that information fills in and remedies anomalous knowledge states, might be misleading to those trained in philosophical debates involving the epistemic claims of naïve empiricism and positivism. The "cognitive" perspective of the LIS tradition, despite its name, is different than the positive, representational assumptions in classical cognitive science and artificial intelligence (AI), lacking its metaphysical understanding of knowledge as representational quasi-entities—what in the philosophy of mind have been termed *qualia*.[3] Where these two traditions do overlap, though, is in seeing information as a product of communicative activities, with cognitive changes in the subject from the reception of a "message" from a document understood as being measurable.

The cognitive turn in LIS, like much of LIS theory and practice, has been rather ambiguously perched between documentation and information science perspectives. In LIS, it is unclear as to whether it is documents or it is their contents that fulfill user information needs and so deserve to have the name of "information."[4]

That there should be more ambiguity to the clear division between the documentation and information traditions than Balnaves and Willson have suggested shouldn't be surprising, since in the modern documentary tradition as a whole it is assumed that documents of all kinds contain contents or "information." Such "epistemic contents" (Frohmann 2004) are often said to be the thoughts of an author that are then communicated to others. Paul Otlet's *Traité de documentation: le livre sur le livre: théorie et practique* (1934) and his earlier and later works, for example, are filled with such an epistemology and its metaphors. For Otlet, the epistemic content fills or "in-forms" (*in-forme*) the material forms of documents. This container-content metaphor for information and its often-accompanying conduit metaphor are common throughout twentieth-century discussions of information. Today even, folk psychology and some perspectives on cognitive science and the philosophy of mind still remain wedded to this type of representational model for knowledge and the mind.

Modern Documentary Structures

From a practical and materialist perspective, what is the difference between documentation and information? From a very general perspective of modern cultural discourse, we may suggest that it is the disappearance from view of the structures and actions of techniques and technologies that mediate documents and users. This disappearance creates the illusion of an immediacy of knowledge, namely, as "information." To be "documented" means to be the object of representation by documents, whereas to be "informed" means to become knowledgeable by the content of information. Documents are constructed *things*, whereas information in ordinary language appears as that which informs us by it being the supposed "content" of documents and people. Successful technical/technological mediation supposedly brings the informational content or essence of persons and things closer together toward successful information retrieval and subsequent mental information transfer.

How are users and information brought together, though? What in the documentary process allows for this supposed transfer of information between documents and persons? Certainly, of course, there is the mutual inscription of information in documents and in persons as users or "needers" at the level of "content" or meaning. That is, the user and the document are brought together under common assumptions of meaningful signs and what should (or should not) be considered to be informative. Before this, though, from the perspective of information systems and information seeking in classical, modernist pre-coordinated systems, at least, there is the function of classification and metadata-naming structures. The function of these systems is to locate the user and the document—sometimes in the case of shelf classification quite literally—next to one another.

Classification and cataloging naming structures and class relationships, however, are not always easily arrived at. Natural language is filled with ambiguities, and it is the function of information professionals to tame this "wild" vocabulary. This is not simply a bibliographic problem, however. Before universal classification structures appeared across library systems in the nineteenth century, zoological taxonomies in the eighteenth century emerged as the necessary a priori functions for the description of natural organisms. Universal bibliographic classifications and descriptions followed the example of zoological taxonomy and classification in the century before them.

As I discussed in the introduction of this book, Suzanne Briet's 1951 book, translated as *What Is Documentation?* (Briet 2006), gives the example of a newly discovered antelope as a primary or initial document, from which secondary (and presumably, tertiary, etc.) documents follow. Briet's example of the antelope shows the similarities between zoological and bibliographic taxonomies. Primary documents are the products of zoological or bibliographic systems, and secondary documents from various discourses take up the figure of the animal, now identified as an antelope, and weighted down under a "vestment of documents" (Briet 2006, 10).

Sylvie Fayet-Scribe (2000) has described the historical organizations in modernity that afforded document organization and retrieval through the adoption of universal standards. It is useful to recall in this regard that Paul Otlet saw the adoption of technical standards as part of international cooperation, leading to the possibility of world peace. Otlet and his colleague Henri LaFontaine not only founded l'Institut international de bibliographie in 1895, but also founded in 1907 the Union of International Associations, devoted to promoting international associations.

In late nineteenth- and early twentieth-century modernity it was seen as important to create international and national standards in order to join peoples with one another, documents with one another, and people with documents. The goal was shared knowledge, shared trade, common languages for communication, and common currencies, universities, governance, and most of all, sharable documents in all textual and nontextual formats. It would perhaps be too much to call this a technological determinism, but not too much to say that the goal was technical embeddedness into all aspects of social life in order to mediate social, cultural, and physical differences. Indeed Briet, in *What is Documentation?*, sees documentation techniques and technologies as a leading force in helping world development in the post–World War II period succeed.

Thus, Otlet and Briet believed that professional documentary organizations and the standardized and standardizing techniques and technologies that came from these had an important role to play in establishing universal forms of information and knowledge, and they hoped that through this universalization group and personal differences could be ameliorated. Modernist documentary techniques and technologies were structures for organizing documents and their textual elements, and these were composed through the expertise of professionals and professional bodies. However, the goal of such organizing was ultimately to serve people's information needs, and so both documents and users were theorized and literally organized by assumptions of what might be considered to be information or knowledge for *types* of users, generally and in discipline-specific domains.

With documentary technical and technological mediation, documents and their textual elements were given universal demarcations so that subjective desires could be effectively and efficiently mediated through these classifying and naming structures toward document and information retrieval. Replacing the nineteenth century "reader" and the overall "reader advisory" services of libraries, the "user" appeared, and the user had to know the terminology and syntax of controlled vocabulary lists, classification structures, and other indexing devices in order to retrieve documents. Such devices represented the contents of the document; they were "about" the contents—"information." Only through such devices could the user ultimately become informed by the documents and only through such could the content and the documents themselves come to be seen as information. Indeed, only through these could a desire or task become an *information need.*

The concept of the user must be seen as a function of the use of indexical retrieval systems (pre-coordinate or post-coordinate, technical or technological) in order to obtain information. Through such systems *both* information (as that which could inform a user) and the user (as he or she "seeking" information by which to become informed) appear as objects and subjects of information systems. In brief, during the modern documentary tradition "mediating" structures between subjects and objects become constructing infrastructures for producing both subjects and objects, ultimately, as we will later examine with social big data, turning both into conjoined data points in parametric indexes.

Historically, though, in theoretical discourse in LIS and for its institutional status, the language of "becoming informed" needed to be reconciled with documentary systems, otherwise the Cutter and Otlet traditions and the two elements of library science *and* information science in the LIS discipline would remain apart. Such a division would echo the practice and research orientations pulling at LIS, the library and other document management traditions on one side and cognitive research into information retrieval on the other. The language of "the user" became a sort of compromise formation, as a synonym for persons on the one hand and as a general category for information (and information system) "use" on the other. But, the biggest rhetorical overlays between these two traditions emerged from the ambiguities of ordinary language: the metonymic slippages among the various meanings of the term "information."

On the one hand, the term "information" refers to documentary forms of all kinds (primary documents, secondary documents, different media and mediums, etc.) and on the other hand "information" refers to the contents, forms, and the epistemic events that these contents and forms of documentary information are supposed to lead to (i.e., "information" in the sense of becoming informed). In order to hold together LIS as a discipline and to hold together the documentary and the communicational paradigms that underlie the historical shift from documents to computer-mediated information retrieval and documentary communication, the term "information" needs to carry a lot of semantic weight.

Michael Buckland's "What Is a Document?" and "Information as Thing"

In contrast to understanding information as an ideational property of a documentary physical or material form, a conceptually broader consideration of information—as a product of the phenomena of informing and becoming informed, while also one linked to documentary practices—can be found in Michael Buckland's well-known articles in LIS, "Information as Thing" (1991) and "What Is a Document?" (1997). From an institutional perspective, Buckland's articles may be read as an attempt to reconcile the two traditions that were dividing LIS by stressing overlaps between the documentary nature of informative items *and* the informative nature of documentary items.

In "Information as Thing" (1991), Buckland offers to disambiguate the term "information" according to three categories: "information-as-process" (the process of becoming informed); "information-as-knowledge" (that which is the product of the process of becoming informed—what traditionally has been referred to as the "content" of documents); and "information-as-thing" (materials, ranging from data to documents, that are said to be informative—that is, again, according to the modern documentary tradition, materials that are said to have informative content). All three of the above are said to be characterized by having the properties of informativeness. Buckland (1991) also tells us that "information-as-thing" is important in information management systems because, essentially, there must be some "thing" for such systems to manipulate. And he then points to some of the discussions that he would later present in "What Is a Document?" (1997)—information as being evidence and information as being any semantically signifying thing, no matter the physical form.

A syllogistic argument underlies Buckland's "Information as Thing": documents inform, what informs is called "information," and so, therefore, documents are information. Information systems deal with physical forms of information/documents and so involve the study of a somewhat distinct form of information from communicative studies. However, as Buckland repeats throughout "Information as Thing," information is something that we *attribute* to objects. Documents/information are social and cultural products, namely, they are evidence of something that is commonly seen to be informative.

In Buckland's article "What Is a Document?" (1997), the notion of "information-as-thing" is developed primarily in terms of Suzanne Briet's discussion of the newly discovered antelope in her book *What is Documentation?* Buckland fills out the notion of evidence in terms of the cultural positioning of the document in systems of signs. This concern with the cultural positioning of the document, as that which contributes to the informativeness of documents and thus makes them to be "information," continues in Buckland's work through "What Kind of Science *Can* Information Science Be?" (Buckland 2012b). In that article he clearly associates information science with cultural and social research, rather than simply with computer science.

Biographically, two events may be highlighted as shaping Buckland's "What Is a Document?": First, he observed a collection of dead woodpeckers at the University of California, Berkeley, Museum of Vertebrate Zoology and then he reflected upon these as documentary collections. And second, explaining this event to W. Boyd Rayward, the historian of European documentation and biographer of Paul Otlet, Buckland received from Rayward the pages from Suzanne Briet's 1951 book, *Qu'est-ce que la documentation?*, which contain in its opening pages her now-famous argument for how a newly discovered antelope can be a document (Buckland 2012a, personal communication).

On the surface, and perhaps most radically for library and bibliographic studies particularly in the early 1990s, Buckland's insight in these articles is that other things than traditional bibliographical forms (e.g., books, journals) may be considered to be documents. This insight was of great importance on the cusp of the broad emergence of digital documents and large-scale networks, which Buckland addressed in a later article, "What is a Digital Document?" (1998). But arguably, what is perhaps Buckland's deeper insight in these articles is his argument, expressed earlier by Buckland's then-colleague Patrick Wilson (1983), that information is whatever is informing or informative. More broad in scope than the cognitive turn in either cognitive science and AI, or in LIS, Buckland's opening up of "informing" and "becoming informed" to a greater material range of evidential forms joined a general economy of information to material documentary types familiar in the LIS tradition. In this way, Buckland's articles express a rather unique compromise between earlier documentary institutions and practices and the post–World War II boom in information science research and practice. In answering the question of *what is a document* in a manner that both preserved the traditional notion of the document as physical evidence and also redefined documents as culturally and socially informing phenomena (rather than as information-bearing forms or materials), the problem of *what is information* was narrowed, avoiding an overly general range of reference for the term (e.g., "information" as a synonym for "stimuli") that would have voided its specificity in regard to information systems and documentary institutions.

Following up on Buckland's claim that consensus is required for something to be considered to be informative, Buckland's articles suggest a historically driven hermeneutic circle between the normative-professional and ordinary-language conceptualizations of information and the events of becoming informed. Those things and types of things that we find to be informative are those (such as information, information systems, information technologies, etc.) that we assume will be informative. Information is what we assume will be informative, and what we assume will be informative is what we consider to be information.

This folding of information into what is informative, and then what is informative into epistemic types, technologies, and events that take on monikers of the term "information" has been explored by others as well (see Bowker 2005). Such issues are social, cultural, political, and sometimes economic, though they are practically mediated and made concrete by what we now think of as information techniques and technologies. This circle of meaning between *being informed* and *information* creates over time intuitive understandings of what is and will likely be informative and thus will yield knowledge. Conversely, it also closes off the past, present, and future to other forms of becoming informed that may not be seen as information. By presenting informing/information and documenting/documentation as cultural, technological, and social expressions (philosophically, "nominal entities"), rather than viewing information and documentation as natural or in a philosophical sense "real entities," Buckland's work opens what might be seen as merely "theoretical" discipline-specific considerations to larger considerations of social, cultural, and technological production, reproduction, and power. In short, viewed from a critical perspective, the discipline of library and information science becomes politicized by virtue of the very language of information.

Summarizing, we might identify here three aspects of Buckland's analysis in the above articles that deserve particular mention. First, Buckland's analysis challenges the ambiguous and confused grammars and conceptualizations of information in both everyday and specialized discourses. In terms of specialized discourses his analysis problematizes theoretical models that are based on ambiguous uses of the term "information," which he argues is used as a "chameleon word" not least in information research and theory and the marketing of information professions (Buckland 2012b). Second, Buckland's articles stress that "information" refers to social, cultural, and technologically mediated types, rather than to natural or "real" entities (see also Frohmann 2004). Third, the articles from the 1990s played a role in mediating the historical shift from documentary systems to information systems in LIS's theoretical discourse and institutional politics. (Though in his 2012 article, Buckland took a strong stand in defense of an LIS field understood as the analysis of the social and cultural use of documents, as distinct from natural or physical notions of the term "information" (Buckland, 2012b).)

Documents and the Creation of Information Needs

Practically, however, the transformation of documentary science to information science had already begun many years before either the cognitive turn in LIS was theorized or before Buckland's analyses in the 1990s. Belkin's ASK and Buckland's concept of "information-as-thing" were theoretical responses to problems in information systems and their use in searching and retrieval. Moreover, the transformation of documentation to information science was taking place through a technical transformation: the shift from pre-coordinate to post-coordinate indexing. This shift marked the importance of the searcher's or user's agency for identifying what was "needed" and what would constitute "information."

Humans are very adaptable, partly because they develop through experience; most technologies are less so, because most technologies are developed through design, in the sense of the teleological implementation of initial forms. As cybernetics after World War II clearly saw, usually adaptation occurs through the agency of the human to the designed machine systems, since the reverse is much harder to create. Humans develop experientially, and this gives them a broad range for learning and adaptation that no machine has yet been able to duplicate as a designed agent. Accordingly, even though post-coordinate, as compared to pre-coordinate, indexing may be seen as an approach that gives the user more freedom for finding the information that he or she wants, it is the transformation of the person into a user (and moreover as a specific type of user, through the selection and narrowing of information choices, often within tasks) that has always been the tool of librarians, ontologists, and search engine designers for raising relevancy scores for searches. This is true whether one is discussing library collection development, classification and cataloging, reader advisory services (where the librarian recommends materials to a reader), special collections, recommending systems, Boolean searching, or even link-analysis search engines, such as Google's PageRank. The notion of a user may differ in scale between all these, but the transformation of persons into users is an essential part of modern information retrieval systems.

Most theories of information retrieval start from the user as an initiator or "cause" of an information need. Documentary information systems *appear* to satisfy an originary information need, but in reality (as can easily been seen in any library reference situation), the choices of various informational entities *produce* a user's specific information need. This is increasingly true when the user is searching *about* a topic (i.e., doing a subject search), rather than doing a direct reference search (what in library science used to be called "ready reference") or a known item search, or when, as is especially the case with Internet searches, the set of possible documents that are being searched through is not readily apparent or is too large to be all present for viewing at one time. In these cases, the winnowing of a desire to a need, of a person to a user, preferably in relation to a task or an interest within a knowledge domain, is imperative from the very beginning of a search, and this is done by the selection and representation of text (or data) and sets of texts (or data) in relation to a priori determined sets of possible relevance. Relevance is determined in pre-coordinate systems according to a priori constructed knowledge domains and privileged search terms. In post-coordinate systems relevance is determined by user input as mediated by user-imposed logical relations (e.g., Boolean searching), by recommendation systems, or by various devices for determining relevance based on either past user behavior and user (semantic, geographical, etc.) context or location, statistical relations between data and metadata elements, or all the above. And above all, relevance is determined by the correct positioning of the subject within naming structures in natural and controlled languages.

So, the key to understanding any user is that of understanding the information system that transforms a text into information and so transforms a person into a user that finds the information system of satisfactory use. The mediating elements of the system are algorithms and other documentary devices that dialectically work with sociocultural norms, such as normative language patterns and psychological assumptions, resulting in indexes of documentary objects and subjects.

As I will argue in the next chapter, in social computing technical algorithms incorporate popular psychological assumptions about knowledge, identity, human relationships, and value. The most important point about all of this is that these indexes point not only to the referential elements of what they mediate, but they also point to "the system itself" (i.e., as a sociotechnical logic) as not only being a hypothetical essence, but also a real existence, courtesy of the system's very usability and success at searching and communicating through technical and technological intermediaries.

Information systems do exist as functional logics, but these logics are not just technical, but sociotechnical. Indexes reference not just the logical and what in philosophy is called the "intensional" elements of the system, but the system itself as a coherent, ideological practice. And it is the deployment of this practice as a set of conceptual or *ideo*logical norms that assures the practicality, the usability, and the success of any information and communication technology system.

In fact, I would suggest that it is the *forgetting* of this ideological and technical/technological dialectic in the infrastructuralization and de-professionalization of documentary structures that underpins the transformation of documentation into information today.

As we saw in the previous chapter, from the very beginnings of modern libraries in the twentieth century the technical/technological elements of information/knowledge organization, selection, and retrieval—that is, becoming informed—were part and parcel of a vision of there being a "world of knowledge." For Otlet, the perfection of human society was achievable by organizing knowledge across the world. But, as Otlet saw, such organization was only possible first by the documentary parsing and representation of texts. *Totality and representation by means of selecting and indexing is the key to the informational dream.* It is a paradoxical, and indeed, a contradictory dream, because it promises the whole based on its fragmentation, reduction, and abstraction. Indeed, "information" in this sense is premised on a social utopia: ultimately, it is being itself that is understood as representation. What is left out of this dream, of course, is an understanding of the human selection and organization of forms for expression; that is, as Buckland (and before him, with a different emphasis, Suzanne Briet) asserts: documentation is a *cultural* technique, though one that also involves the enfolding of social norms as well as cultural forms, into these techniques and use. The reproducibility of sociocultural norms and forms constitutes political economy. It is precisely cultural forms, along with social norms, in their broadest range of expression (from language to taste) that contemporary search engine companies, such as Google, wish to capture and technically manipulate and (re)deploy in order to meet systems (including economic, social, and political systems) requirements and needs.

But, before we enter more fully into a discussion of the indexicality of contemporary social computing in the next chapter, I would like to examine the predecessor to this in scholarly citation indexing and citation analysis. Citation indexing and analysis are an important moment in the transition from a strictly documentary to an informational episteme along lines of what we see appear today, namely, social and communicative computing. Citation indexing and analysis are a professionalized, rudimentary, and microscopic version of the social computing algorithms that we popularly use today. Historically, they arise out of printed citation indexes and continue to use documentary forms of representation. They constitute a bridge between documentation and social computing. And historically, in LIS and in the wider world of information management and its research, they were an important transition point from document retrieval to a retrieval based on a representational "aboutness" mediated by the social valorization of computerized processes of indexing—that is, to an *information retrieval*.

With scholarly citation indexing and analysis and its extension into webmetrics and other altmetric analyses we see a political economy of sociotechnically mediated value creation for documents and persons, which indexes not just work that has been published, but which indexes—and through this comes to characterize—sociological and personal forms and identities for scholarly work. In other words, citation indexes themselves are informational objects in the sense that they both create their referents and trace the political economies through which they appear. By highlighting the problem of a *theoretical* account for citation indexing and analysis, I hope to bring the relation of citation indexing and analysis and political economy into the open.

Citation Indexing and Citation Analysis

Modern scholarly citation analysis follows from scholarly citation indexing. Eugene Garfield began the Institute for Scientific Information (ISI) with what would become the Science Citation Index to which was later added the Social Science Citation Index and the Arts and Humanities Index, as well as several additional indexes, which today is altogether known as the product, *Web of Knowledge*, owned by Thomson Reuters. Today, this collection of scholarly citation indexes has been joined by Scopus and Google Scholar. As can be seen by some of their names, the attempts of such indexes have been to show scholarly communication beginning with journals in the sciences. The attempt to do this through metrical means forms the area of study of bibliometrics, which today has expanded into scientometrics and other types of documentary metrics. Though citation indexing has expanded into the humanities, the use of citation analysis in the humanities for academic tenure and promotion evaluation has been limited by both sociological factors (for example, the still strong role of personal evaluation) and by relatively incomplete indexing by the major scholarly indexes (when compared to the sciences). It should be added that across all the disciplines, claims about the evidentiary use of citations may be misleading, too, because of the rather common use of citations by scholars to build up their own academic capital (e.g., gratuitous citation), rather than for providing evidence in support of an argument. Conversely, leaving out these social and cultural factors can lead to an incomplete and rationalized picture of citation behavior.

Some leaders in citation analysis and bibliometrics, such as Blaise Cronin, have long asked why a theory of citation analysis has been so hard to arrive at (Cronin 1984). Though the idea that a theory of such a practice is even needed is not universal within information science discourse, the core questions that lead to a desire for such a theory are intriguing and telling: What does citation indexing socially do and what does citation analysis show?

Starting from the latter question, one could come up with many answers to this question based on the literature. One could say that citation analysis shows: the influence of a work and of a scholar on subsequent work; it shows the influence of a work in a discipline; it shows the citing behavior of scientists and scholars; it shows networks of influence and co-authorship; it shows core and more marginal subjects and authors in disciplines; it shows research disciplines and their subdomains and their relationships to one another; and it shows the major or minor producers of works in a discipline and their relations as shown by citations. The claim to represent social behavior through practices of citing seems to constitute the explanatory basis of citation analysis and its social reason for being. Citation indexes are core devices for supporting these claims.

Citations show these behaviors through counting and indexing documentary forms, such as books and journals, as well as by counting and indexing documentary fragments and representations, such as author names, titles of works, and other vocabulary taken from a document. As a social science practice, it claims through correlational regularities to show and predict social behaviors.

But, the social sciences have always had a peculiar relationship to what they claim to represent. The social sciences involve a hermeneutic or interpretive circle with the subjects that they are observing and describing. Whether similar or different from the types of people that the researchers are, researchers cannot simply take their subjects of study as objects. Despite the use of methods and techniques to mediate judgments, it is still judgments—of behavior, reasons, and intentions—that are being read upon other human beings in the choice of research, in the taxonomies used to structure research and theory, and in the understanding of results. Such judgments need not be attributed to simply individual researchers, but occur through the language that is used to describe other people and their behavior, reasons, and intentions, as well as the techniques and methods chosen. In short, the social sciences ultimately involve subjects studying subjects; not subjects studying objects. The criteria for "object-ive" studies used in the physical sciences, such as asserting causal rather than correlational regularities, replicable experiments, universality of explanations, and prediction, are often inapplicable in the social sciences where the behavior and expression of human beings make up the topics of research.

Seen from the standpoint of the physical sciences, the social sciences remain haunted by the problem of the nature of the reality that they show: Is it an object-ive reality or is it merely the re-presentation by scientific methods and rhetorical form of the grammatical and/or logical properties of the terms that frame the study? In other words, does the experiment do anything other than to technically and methodologically operational-ize its founding assumptions? These founding assumptions are located in not only the contemporary and historical discourses and taxonomies of a field of research, not only in its methods and techniques and technolo-gies of research, but also in the folk knowledge or folk psychologies that have often drifted into the epistemic assumptions of social science research paradigms and agendas. Discursive and conceptual metaphorical and met-onymical borrowings are unavoidable elements of social science discourse and research, which are sometimes undetected because the focus of the sci-ence is upon empirical, rather than a priori, research.

So, for example, the conduit metaphor of language, Claude Shannon's statistical information transfer model, and computational symbol manipu-lation—these all have drifted into being different models for human com-munication and thought through the trope of "information." The critical onus on showing the validity of these drifts cannot be found in empirical experiments (which are inscribed in these assumptions as the framework for their a posteriori "empirical" activities), but in a priori epistemological and historical studies (which are usually kept outside of the framework of scien-tific research—institutionally, methodologically, and rhetorically). At best, empirical work can only summon us to problematic a priori assumptions.

Thus, citation analysis, like many other social science practices, remains problematic as to what it actually shows and explains. If "showing" is strictly meant at a mechanical level of prescription and engineering (e.g., showing how to do technical research with better efficiency), then the question of what it is that citation analysis socially explains is nullified, and it loses its validity as a social science practice. If "showing" means, primarily, a social representation, then a social theory of citation analysis is useful for both explaining and guiding the practice toward social explanations rather than simply bettering engineering practices. The problem of having a citation analysis theory, then, is *not* a secondary consideration to the practice of citation analysis and the building of citation indexes that allow such analysis. "Analysis" in this sense is a problem of explaining something through a theoretical framework. Theory guides the analysis. Citation indexes and their use in analysis are the chief technical means that afford such. *The techniques and technologies of the citation index enfold the social theory and value of citation analysis within their algorithms and their production of indexical lists and relationships*, which are then used for social and institutional evaluations. Through this means, citation indexes show themselves to be culturally valuable and socially useful.

The problem, then, of what it is that citations socially do is central to the construction of citation indexes. Citation indexes index certain metadata categories and documentary fragments and representations (author, title, subject, publication, date, etc.) in order to provide an explanation of something; that something is often said to be social relationships in the scientific practice. The indexes must be designed not only in order to help explain, but also more importantly, to facilitate and further prescribe the further indexing of persons to persons, documents to documents, and persons to the document that each citation shows.

If citation indexes help citations show social relationships through indexing select parts of the document, then, what is it about citations that allow this showing to occur in the first place? In other words, is there something about citations that helps us understand citation indexes? Is there a theory of citations that allows us to understand what it is that citation indexes index—what they point to and coordinate—in the social sphere?

Henry Small, who worked for many years at the Institute for Scientific Information (ISI) and who specializes in citation analysis, published a paper in 1978 titled, "Cited Documents as Concept Symbols" (Small 1978), which attempted to provide a citation theory that explained citation in terms of reference. It is an important paper that can help us answer these questions.

For Small, citations are "concept symbols" not only for documents or for fragments or representations of documents, but for their ideas. Citing Edmund Leach's *Culture and Communication: The Logic by which Symbols are Connected. An Introduction to the Use of Structuralist Analysis in Social Anthropology* (Leach 1976), Small's article argues that the citing of a text by another text constitutes the "metaphorical" or "metonymical" transfer of ideas between them. Starting with the claim that the notion of "symbol" refers to a representation of the physical document referred to, as well as to its ideas, Small extends into citation theory what he reads as Leach's "metaphorical" and "metonymical" relationships (that is, in terms of the faithfulness by which citation reproduces the ideas from one text to another, with "metaphorical" connoting less, and "metonymical" more, faithfulness):

The kind of relationships between the document (consisting of pages) and its sign (consisting of author, journal, volume, page, year) is in Leach's terminology "metonymic"—that is, there are physically shared characteristics. The relationship between the cited document and the concept it symbolizes, on the other hand, is "metaphoric." In the extreme, this means that there need not be any similarity between the document and the concept it stands for—or to put it more directly, the perceived content of a document is independent of the document itself. This is an overstatement of the case, because certainly in most cases the document contains the ideas which it comes to symbolize. To the extent that it does, the relationship between cited document and concept is also "metonymic" (for example, when a direct quote is made from the cited document). (Small 1978, 329)

Then, in a gesture that completes the Saussurean structural analysis that underlies his paper, Small writes,

I also follow Leach in regarding an "idea" in its written form in a scientific paper as an imperfect "copy of an original" which resides in the mind of an individual. In the case of "standard symbols," the "idea" is the product of a dialogue and selection process on the part of many individuals over a period of time. It follows that any single actor's utterance cannot be used to reconstruct the "standard symbol": we can achieve this only by aggregating many utterances. One of the hypotheses to be explored in this paper is that a scientist carries with him a repertoire of such collective concepts and their corresponding document-symbols. These are his tools-of-the-trade, and provide the conceptual and methodological framework for his work. (Small 1978, 329)

Small's observations about "metaphor" and "metonymy" in citation practices start from the understanding that evidence needs to be evidence *about* something. What that something is, allows the transfer of "ideas" to take place between one document and another, and so allows that a citation is a "symbol." That commonality is the "third term"—the discourse, vocabulary, and logic (i.e., the "grammar")—by which the two texts are held together. That grammar is made up of the physical or material marks, which reference one document to another within a practice of citation. But Small, interestingly, also sees that metadata—cited names, volumes, and so forth—are not the essence of citation reference. What is essential to citation reference is a reference to ideas. These ideas share a language and, most faithfully, a similarity of reference and discourse.

In other words, citations are not only symbols nor are citation indexes only the process of technical calculations. They are manifestations of social processes of distributing ideas. What are ideas? Ideas or concepts are words or other symbols that are capable of being put into action by people, either with other such symbols or in relation to the physical world, or both, as meaningful expressions. That is, they are meaningful signs from which we infer intentions and relationships.

Small (1987) argues that, "the 'idea' is the product of a dialogue and selection process on the part of many individuals over a period of time." Corresponding to Saussure's notion of *langage*, language (here, scholarly discourse) is made up of enunciations from a hypothetical *langue* (here, bodies of concepts or "ideas" in that discourse, which are actualized as real entities by their repetition as enunciations—*parole*). Seen from a social perspective, citation is an act of not just attributing, but of drawing from and contributing, to broad socio-cultural or a disciplinary toolboxes of concepts ("tools of the trade").

Small (1987) is here articulating a concept of knowledge as tools for performing professional, specialized, acts. The text is the researcher's expression of his or her own toolbox of skills as a professional self, built out of both larger sociocultural and professional toolboxes of ideas, methods, vocabulary, techniques, and technologies. Citation is the means for acknowledging and supporting a researcher's tools by means of referencing an already published, and so public, knowledge. Citations not only keep previously published documents from vanishing from the public record, but they also attach conceptual attributes to a physical document. When all is said and done, it is the *reading* of ideas into and out of texts that constitutes the *intellectual reality* of the texts, which in turn is what keeps the physical document and its bibliographic attributes in view of researchers, rather than merely being of interest to bibliographers or others interested in the bibliographic attributes for their own sake.

In sum, Small (1987) is claiming that what citations show is what we might call the conceptual traces of a discipline's political economy of knowledge; that is, what in Marxist terms is called *ideology*—the rationality or logic of ideas that is shown by the regularity and force of their expression and deployment. The two temporal and spatial moments of such expressions are that of authorial enunciations on the one hand and a potential body of knowledge awaiting citation on the other hand. Citation analysis occurs because these two poles continually reconstitute one another in a metonymic, dialectical exchange in what becomes seen as patterns of influence. But, it is also such a production of reproduction (Althusser 2001) that allows a certain ideological form in a political economy to be traced, although not without differences, over time.

The self can be understood as a hypothetical, but nevertheless real, toolbox of learned skills, which forms a subset of available concepts and skills circulating in culture and society (Harré 1989). The self is, in this sense, a psychological or experiential index (Day 2007). Ideally, the corresponding technological index for such would not be a top-down set of categories for "tool selection" from the available literature, but would be tailored to the self's needs, as a self within certain conditions of situated speech. Such an ideal index would include not only the formal terms for indexing and use (e.g., title, subject, author, and abstract), but would include devices for directing the search to a user, as he or she would be constituted as a subject of need in a given sociocultural situation and time. That is to say, algorithms would personalize search by creating technical indexes that would reference citations to psychological experience and social positioning.

What we've been describing, of course, are those social computing algorithms that today attempt to create personalized searching. Recommendation and recursive social algorithms make use of live social psychologies for refining the indexing or the documentary social positioning of the self. They "aid" the self in that positioning by helping to determine the types of cultural and social tools that the self decides to deploy in given documentary-mediated situations. Technological indexes are, then, not simply convenient tools for searching, but they are technical extensions of the self that then also reinforce the development of selves according to the contents of those indexes.

If the self is a toolbox of skills, then knowledge constitutes certain types of expressions of skills, namely, skills of knowing (which include vocabulary, concepts, modes of expression, etc.). What constitutes knowing depends upon the set and kinds of expressive acts that are socially accepted and seen as "knowledge." One has knowledge only in so far as one can perform acts of knowing. The substantive form, "knowledge," at least in regard to its cognitive meaning, refers to a hypothetical mental set of tools and their expressive use, actualized in performances, certificates, and other performative acts (Day 2007).

Indexes are knowledge management systems in the sense that they systematically manage knowledge, both in the sense of its being understood as potential expressions issuing from documents and from persons. As we see with citation indexing and analysis and with their social use, algorithms and the indexes that mediate the subject's seeking, and the object's meaning and value, play a key role in documentary modernity for determining what can be seen as knowledge and what can be seen as the knowing "self" and the knowledgeable "person." (In the technical sense according to Rom Harré (1989), that the term "self" refers to unique, hypothetical sets of potential expressions, and the term "person" refers to summary observations of the self's actual performances understood within cultural and social norms.)

Thus, a theory of citation, as Small puts it,

if such a theory is possible, must take account of the symbolic act of authors associating particular ideas with particular documents. The analysis has shown that when a scientist cites, he or she is creating a link between a concept, procedure, or kind of data, and a document or documents. In some cases the association of idea and document is well established by uniform practice within the community (Leach's "standard symbol"). Recurring patterns of terminology used by citing authors when referring to these documents show that they have become standardized in their usage and meaning. In other cases, the individual author (scientist) may be making the association for the first time and the document-idea connection remains in the realm of private symbols (Leach's "nonce symbols"). (Small 1987, 337)

In reality, however, there are no exclusively "private symbols," or at least any that can be meaningful by others. Meaningful knowledge means knowledge that is drawn out of and contributes back to to *langue*—social or professional toolboxes. The personal expression of an author is informed by this, and so, subsequently, all meaningful texts are, by definition, to various degrees public knowledge (even in the case of diaries, autobiographies, etc.), that is, symbols that are understandable, even by the author him or herself at some other time or circumstance.

The critical question for a theory of citation analysis, though, is how citations and citation indexes inform. Once again the question occurs: How do texts and human beings become coordinated with one another as documents and users, so that a representational linkage and heritage may be established and strike others as "true"?

If citations are seen not only as central tools in the practices of creating "idea symbols," but also as symbols of the political economies of citation behavior in academic and scientific research, then we may see citations and citation indexing as constituting an important technical logic in the sociotechnical practice of scholarly knowledge and academic and scientific career advancement.

In traditional scholarly citation practices texts are indexed as documents according to metadata and fragments of bibliographic data. With traditional citation indexing systems this relatively small amount of information guides the indexing of and research into the relation of persons and persons, documents and documents, and persons and documents, but it leaves many questions unanswered regarding their relationships (e.g., influence? gratuitous citation?), which are reflected in the many questions about the social behavior and purpose for citations that haunt the theorization of citation analysis. The bare outlines of a political economy are evident, though: Knowledge comes from scholarly documents (i.e., documents that have been included in citation indexing), it has a history that moves "forward" and "backward" in time (influence), it has domains and subdomains (that can be established by subject metadata and semantic derivation from bibliometric data), it has authorship (single or multiple authors), and so forth. This political economy reflects the technical logic of the metadata and the algorithms that construct the scholarly citation indexes (and, of course, the privileged categories in the bibliographic tradition that shape machine-aided citation indexing, and thus, their analyses).

Citations occur as knowledge through their position within traditions and disciplines. They produce the reproduction of those traditions and disciplines in their very act of citation and in their being indexed and in those indexes being used. (Although not without difference, not without "progress"; in citation the *Aufhebung* of dialectic moves "forward" and "backward" in time, as a line of influence.) Therefore, citations are tokens of a sociotechnical rationality wherein disciplinary subjects and objects are formed through technical indexes, which are traces of the social reproduction of what is thought to be information or not, knowledge or not.

Citation indexes, and not just their records, contain "ideas." Their "ideas" are a product of a dialectic between their technical/technological means and the ideological universe that they are mediating and reasserting by the use of the cultural forms and the social rules of citation. Again, this ideological universe is made up of cultural forms and social norms, which result in reproduced practices and values, which together we call "political economy." Citation indexes are not just a device for measuring, but for reproducing, the means of production of the values that they supposedly show. Like citations, they are not just technical, but sociotechnical; they enfold and reproduce sociocultural systems of values and norms.

In the next chapter we will look at citation indexes on a much more vast scale of knowledge, information, and persons than simply scholarly communication.

4 Social Computing and the Indexing of the Whole

Pre- and post-coordinate indexes, and the social techniques and the documentary and computational algorithms that help create them, are central for not only bringing into appearance texts as documents and information, but they also bring into appearance selves as personal identities that are known by their digital expressions. As with Suzanne Briet's antelope (Briet 2006), an identity as an identifiable *something* in modernity often appears through a documentary process. This documentary, ontological function may take place with or without the participation of the being or thing involved, using a priori or a posteriori techniques or algorithms of identity assignment, and these may be explicit or implicit in the systems within which persons/things appear as identities. In the classic scholarly citation systems, for example, we arrive at documentary identity and value—upon persons and texts—by the indexing of metadata and documentary fragments within political economies of value and use (through privileged bibliographic categories such as author, title, subject, etc.). Social computing expands the quantitative functions and the social values of such systems beyond academic and scholarly institutions and gives greater weight (metaphorically, and literally in terms of the technical functions of algorithms) to sociological and psychological values functioning in the social networks of the documentary items. As with Google PageRank, with its relevancy-based link-analysis algorithm, citation indexing and analysis is introduced *into the corpus* of what is searchable by the user, making the search more contemporary, rather than simply retrospective. Here, the social becomes a much more integrated and *infrastructural* component of the search, folded within the actual algorithms and the resulting indexes, rather than staying in the convergence of bibliographical metadata and social values for these (Rieder 2012).[1] Thus, what makes social computing social is not just the technical and technological software and hardware, nor even that these are used by large groups of people, but rather, that both these components are enfolded into one another so that social and psychological needs are fulfilled by the machines, and the machines train the users and so reinforce certain social and psychological mores. "Usefulness," in the sense of fulfilling "information needs" is the chief end of social computing, and so it forms yet another moment in the modern documentary tradition.

Today on the Internet, through more advanced algorithms and indexing techniques and technologies, "texts" (understood broadly to mean human-understood inscriptions), and persons and other beings are made into documentary identities. Authors and other types of individuals are asserted by names, personal qualities are asserted by a person's "likes" and "dislikes," social contacts, previous searches, and other attributions; and, human and non-humans are made into media personalities (e.g., videos of Henri, "the existentialist cat," making the rounds in 2012 and 2013) by their popular indexing within documentary cultural and social economies. Newer computer-mediated post-coordinate searching and algorithms introduce a greater ability to develop time-valued and space-sensitive social and cultural inferences. Through recursive and social algorithms historical and social dimensions to the documentary subject's knowledge are added.

Social computing indexes are not in any simple way *either* social or technical, since their sociotechnical characteristics are products of a dialectical interaction between the algorithmic calculation of sociocultural norms, on the one hand, and on the other, the actual practical use of social computing algorithms and indexing. Recursive and social algorithms add historical and social dimensions into the formal and cultural mediation of documents and persons that characterized earlier twentieth-century modern documentation techniques and technologies. Documentation is not now only a "cultural technique" (Briet 2006), but it is an historical and social technique that performs the relatively "live" indexical positioning of subjects.

Recursive algorithms, which take account of past searches and combine these with social production in order to then prompt or otherwise offer documentary choices to the subject "anew" lead to a dialectical gathering up or subsumption (*Aufhebung*: Hegel and Marx's term) of previous tendencies into new past, present, and future possibilities while excluding, marginalizing, and making extinct other potentialities. This is one of the bases for the somewhat paradoxical and surprising phenomenon of the narrowing, rather than the expanding, of resources, as well as the information needs of persons, during Internet searching. The early popular hope of the Internet, like Otlet's hope with his Mundaneum, was that information technologies would lead to social harmony. But instead, what we have seen is that they just as often lead to greater factionalization as people's "information needs" are met and reinforced by recursive and socialized documentary systems.

Social computing socializes and historicizes the self into entities of personal expression, akin to the transformation of texts into documents. Here, the mediation of persons into users and of texts into documents that began in the epistemic-historical moment of documentation advances fully into an informational stage, slightly foreshadowing and working alongside the social big data reduction both of documentary subjects and objects to become conjoined data points for possible and predictable expressions. Subjects are represented as "about" not only their "knowledge states" but also about their documentary histories (in search, or in any other documentary regime, such as credit histories).

Computational Information Infrastructures

The transition from classic documentation metadata structures to computational information infrastructures as mediators of texts and persons can be explained in many ways and by many technologies, but citation analysis provides a direct historical link between document management and social computing systems. The development of Google PageRank's link analysis algorithm was influenced, for example, by Eugene Garfield's Science Citation Index along with sociometrics (Rieder 2012). More generally, social network analysis and techniques, such as link analysis, has expanded the scale of citation indexing beyond scholarly domains.

The effects of this transition can be seen in the creation of broader social identities ("online identities"), as well as scholarly ones, as products of the everyday adoption of the sociotechnology of social computing systems. In scholarly citation analysis, markers of social value, such as the h-index, are used within an economy of academic evaluation and value determination. Likewise journal impact factors for journal value determination also shape the value of scholars, though indirectly. Qualities and values are predicated upon persons through these technical systems and personal qualities and values are then increasingly determined in the evaluation of scholars by the academic system in terms of these predications. Selves are turned into scholarly persons, and increasingly, are commoditized along lines of past production and recognition, as determined by citation indexes working with and being analyzed by citation analyses, which in turn are answering questions that are important for forms of political economy. Again, the technical/technological components are "useful" only in so far as they fold into their algorithms social and cultural values in action, that is, in so far as they fold in political economies.

The algorithms don't simply run alongside ideology, but rather, they are designed into ideology, which is to say also, conversely, that ideology is enfolded into the logic and elements of calculative devices. Algorithms and indexes aren't *just* coincidental *agencements* or parts of sociotechnical assemblages, but rather these assemblages develop within parts of political economy, whether through the sponsorship or action of research programs, personal sponsors, corporations, state institutions, venture capital, or simply market directives, so as to be expressions that are useful to some parts of these founding and directing institutions, as well as to personal users.

Social computing takes the modern documentary mediation and creation of sociotechnical dialectics further in two ways: the recursive (Thomas 2012) historicization and the broader socialization of information needs, and the a posteriori empiricalization of persons and texts as sociocultural historical information through these. Through recursive software and social network analyses, as well as through more traditional documentary devices and affordances, persons and texts become historically and socially indexed and profiled in new and sometimes peculiar manners. Thanks to the widespread and infrastructural presence of these documentary tools, what began as analogical documentary characterizations of historical and social relationships (e.g., credit "histories" and Facebook "friends") has gradually come to replace the traditional senses of such relationships. And, as is often the case, what have been left behind with the triumph of the modern documentary tradition are the time-consuming, interpretative, and judgmental elements of human relationships to other human beings, one's self, other beings as a whole, and texts.

As Briet wrote in 1951 (Briet 2006), documentation is a cultural specialization that uses information and communication techniques and technologies to serve and produce new social and cultural rhythms. For Briet, these rhythms follow the score of modernity as a progressive history of the expansion of scale for technically and technologically mediated documentary understandings. Since Briet's time, that rhythm has both sped up even more and has covered nearly the entirety of life, from our social to our psychological lives to our ability to perform research and work and to be entertained. Indeed, it isn't just "science" that modern documentary techniques and technologies and documentalists serve and lead, but rather, ideology and political economy, as these are embedded in both professional and everyday use.[2] Technologies and political economy reproduce one another through *design*—the design of future machines to serve human beings and human beings being shaped to work with new technologies. Modern information and communication technologies are, above all, *devices and systems that function through both sociocultural and technical logics.*

In contrast to the past orientation of pre-coordinate indexing (say in regard to indexed vocabulary), current information algorithms and infrastructures are more socially present and even future oriented. They gather together past searches in order to subsume them within present searches and shape future searches (which then mediate the past), and this historical mediation is also remediated by a user's social networks and larger trends. Personal needs and the needs of others, concrete documentational, informational, and data materials and ideational realms of language, expectations, and normative meanings (ideology) form the general system of past, present, and future expressions that information and communication systems are built to serve and evolve. They are *practical* systems, in the sense that they serve needs, and they are idealized systems in the sense that they reproduce those needs in progressively historicized and socialized forms (and so, too, reinforce their own sociotechnical designs).

The informational character of social computing may be understood through Hegelian dialectics. Dialectics, in the sense that we are using the term here, refers to the rational—the "meaningful"—emergence of subjects and objects over time through a systemic logic according to a governing concept of being. In dialectics, a concept of being as well as a logic for its unfolding are *essential* to the emergence of the subjects and objects involved. But a concept of being and its logic also gradually comes to an existent *appearance* through the phenomena of subjects and objects in their historical relationships, and through becoming who and what they are as meaningful and valued entities according to the system in which they are inscribed and expressing. The concept is enfolded within social and personal needs, and so appears over time as the essence of those needs themselves through expressed personal desires performed through a culture's expressive forms and social norms. Persons expressing themselves as the spirit of their age give the concept of an age a reality.

The sociocultural system mediates the purely logical forms of techniques and technologies in order to give them the quality of being *useful*. And, on the other hand, technical and technological devices are designed as being *useful* by enfolding in their functional expressiveness the social and cultural assumptions that will make them meaningful and valuable for the human environment in which they are located.

What we search for is what something or some persons are said to be *about*, often in contemporary culture and psychology then positioning ourselves in regard to them, either for or against, either in curiosity or repulsion, liking, disliking, recommending, or simply being disinterested in and disregarding them. Informationally, that is, in modern documentary psychology, I am for-others as they are for-me, only in so far as I *am* and they *are*. Insofar as my needs come from my own social positioning as a person, then it is the "they" that gives to me the characteristics of my I, but an "I" that is always a "me" just as the others are a "they." Through documentary mediation, my "I" is a me that is mediated by or given as data. The documentary given (the "information" or the "data") is, in the Lacanian sense, *moi*—it *is* me (Day 2013); it is my appearance through the documentary given—the melding of dominant personal and social psychology and technologies of documentary organization and retrieval. And for the information system, I am less the self and more the "me"—a "me" among other *moi*. Through the Internet we come to experience not only others, but *types* of our own individual selves, as objects of our contemplation as never before in history. And conversely, the Internet may become a forum for masquerade, social positioning, and the types of ironic literary and visual tropes that work against this, but largely without managing to escape the psychologies and political economies governing popular culture. While local phenomenon may escape this rule, as one scales up, as local political tensions become "viral" for example, and as mediating documentary algorithms and indexes further position textual and personal subjects, the force of normative cultural psychology and politics often comes to rein in the more "radical" moments of personal and social transformation.

Instrumental rationality—usefulness—positions others and one's self correctly in what is understood to be the present and only political economy. Pragmatically viewed, such objectivity is seen as both natural and necessary. Politically, socially, and morally, one *must see one's self as being* just one being among many in order to be judged objectively. Through this objectivity, self-consciousness becomes mature, as the self positions itself correctly within the normative categories of personhood.

In a documentary society, from the viewpoint of all the others, I am just another. This is a lesson that we most have learned, both analogically and experientially, from the worldwide growth of the Internet and from neoliberalism, and it is why the existential self that emerged from out of the Romantic reaction to industrialism now has become increasingly fragile. I am another by such a name (e.g., "Ron Day" or another proper name), with the same mortal conditions as the other, thrown to compete for survival with the others in the arena of "the market." I appear on various documentary markets, in ways that I can try to manage according to the wishes that I may have for my public appearance. The photograph of me on an Internet site is different from an old photograph kept in a drawer. The former context presents more of a problem of my self-positioning in a public documentary space than the latter.

Yet, along with the others, and along with algorithms and indexes, I am also one who is reading and interpreting such. The splitting and the dialectic of the subject remains, but the subject is now burdened more with its objectivity; not just as a moment in the subject's consciousness, but as the subsuming logic that increasingly drives the subject's consciousness of itself and others, courtesy of documentary evidence. While in Heidegger's *Being and Time* (published in 1927) the finitude of the other is the condition by which one finds a commonality with the others, resulting in solicitude and care—as well as anxiety in regard to one's own finitude—the same sympathy in neoliberalism leads to feelings of competition, aloneness, resentment, and failure. And on the Internet, as with all media personalities, many people never die, but instead maintain an afterlife as a document. The nature of the awareness or feeling of being with others—that is, how *Dasein* and *Mitsein*, as *modalities of being are ontically expressed and experienced*—depends upon the political economy within which the subject appears. Though the subject may find and extend care and solicitude through social networks, the documentary push of the Internet in this day often moves such interactions toward cursory "likes" or "dislikes," thumbs up or thumbs down, before moving onto the next documentary task.

We want to know *about something or someone*, some object or some person, and the index provides a means to do this through the organization and representation of documents. Wanting to know *about*, in the documentary sense, is wanting to understand something or someone within the context of a system of knowledge, that is, to know it or them as evidence within some taxonomy or discourse we are working with. This something or someone *appears* through its being a sign within a system of reference. It is pointed to (extensional reference) through an *indice*, but this indexical sign, when brought under critical analysis, also signifies the system or discourse through which it appears (what in philosophy is termed "intensional" reference). Informational objects inform us as to their extensional referent *and* to their systems of representation.

This individual ("x") is a *dog*, and *dogs* belong to families of animals (in a taxonomical sense) and to families of people (in a sense of dog ownership or companionship). There are working dogs, cuddly dogs, and there are angry dogs. *This dog is a* loving dog or *this dog is* an angry dog. (This woman/man will make a good mate, this woman/man will not, etc.) The indexical sign points to an extensional referent, but this referent is a sign in as much as it belongs to categories of meaning and environments of sense. We learn the categories when we learn the words, but we understand their meaning better (or only) when we learn their sense, as well. (Just as a number becomes meaningful to us only by understanding it within a mathematical syntax or seeing it in some practical use.) All signs that have meaning and sense are indexical, which is to say that all humanly affected signs are indexically placed, amid constellations of other signed things (whether they be empirical or fantastic). Phenomenologically, the thing or being appears to us from out of documentary relationships that are learned through experience. All identities, including our own as existents, are signs that are meaningful only through other signs (and so must be developmentally or experientially learned) (Day 2007).

The problem with documentary categories is that it may appear that experience or reading and interpretation, understanding and judgment, are no longer necessary, that what is given by the information or data is a "fact": that the constellation of references is closed, that the text is closed and is a document.

However, the modern sense of the term "information," as a family of discourses of representation, remains, despite its current prominence, a galaxy amid other galaxies of knowledge. It is given, historically, socially, and culturally, through a political economy that manifests itself in the intersection of *techne* and language, namely through that sociotechnical concept of "information technology." Such a concept, as I have been stressing throughout this book as throughout my other works, has values and deployments that involve symbolically unfolding futures as well as rereadings of the past and the present in terms of its dominant episteme. Thus, if we still accept the charge of *critique*, it is politically necessary and responsible to examine the logics and rationality by which the historical and social unfolding of concepts and technologies of information and knowledge occur. These unfold and enroll within a systemic logic; this logic is not exclusionary, however, but rather maintains its difference within a universe filled with other values for knowledge and identity. Its dominance or not follows an historical course that is a play of forces of power; those forces index the potentialities (both the determinate and the generative powers) of the present and future of this episteme, and of the potential powers of its agents and concepts.

Within a certain philosophical context, we may briefly pose the issue in the following manner: In Lockean empiricism and subsequent empirical positivism, objects are viewed as having an integral self- or "auto-affective" presence outside of cognition and have the ability to affect consciousness through such presence. In contrast, the Kantian critique of empiricism viewed objects as being structured as known things by categories of the understanding. Subsequently, however, Hegelian dialectics, emerging from German speculative idealism of the late eighteenth and early nineteenth centuries, viewed the construction of categories of the understanding (starting not the least from consciousness or the subject itself in its self-understanding), as emergent out of an experience with others that lie both within and outside of the subject's consciousness. Attempting to advance beyond Kant's critiques through a phenomenological account of consciousness's experience in the world, consciousness was historicized as the subject, but in this, it was also made to be an explicit social, cultural, and in sum, political, subject; that is, a subject of a governing and historically realized political idea or concept. The subject was not simply historical, but rather, its historical quality was that of an expression of the spirit of a governing "age" or "society." And since all governing concepts are realized only by their success and usefulness, this is to say that the subject emerges as a product of political economy and the regulation and repressions or expressions of potential and possible forces of power.

The historicization of Kant's epistemology through a dialectical account of experientially formed consciousness can be found in Hegel's *Phenomenology of Spirit* (*Phänomenologie des Geistes* 1807), where consciousness becomes self-conscious through viewing itself through that which it initially appears as not being. According to a "closed" dialectic or "right" Hegelianism, subjects discover what they are through otherness and, most extremely, through the alienation of being treated as objects (as in Hegel's famous master-slave dialectic in the *Phenomemology*). A more "open" dialectic or sometimes "left" Hegelianism stresses the force of the dialectic as historical becoming, rather than stressing subjects and objects as foundational ontological positions. Here, subjects and objects, subjectivity and objectivity (including persons understood as objects), are moments in the becoming of personal self-consciousness within and as part of the historical unfolding of being as a certain historical and sociocultural idea or concept of being. Here, consciousness or the subject is but a moment in the development of self-consciousness as a certain type of subject within a certain concept and logic of being. The subject is subjected to the governance of an essential idea or concept, which guides personal and social development and defines an age.

On the one hand, from the perspective of the Hegelian universal, a concept of being historically unfolds and the subject comes to understand itself though the notion and logic of that concept. (For example, the historical logic that concerns us in this book, of course, is that of the subject knowing itself through and as documentary evidence—in late modernism, understood by the term "information.") On the other hand, from the perspective of the Hegelian "particular," *Geist* ("spirit" or "mind" in English) is the personal desire that is historically worked out through a relationship to the other. In this working out of desire the self expresses itself through actions and comes to be seen and comes to see itself through these actions as both self and person, subject and other, hypothetical set of powers and recognized sets of powers. As participating in the spirit of his or her time, the particular individual develops and acts within historically specific cultural forms and social norms, which in turn fit within larger ideologies and traditions of beliefs (what one could call "metaphysical traditions").

Within an historical concept and its episteme, a concept of being is actualized in the actions of people acting within the spirit of their age. The role of ideology is to unconsciously govern these actions through the regulation of cultural forms and social norms within moral and political economies so as to allow the spirit of the age its greatest expression possible. Through ideology, as through physical force, discipline, and punishment (the "repressive state apparatus," see Althusser 2001), other potentialities—past, present, and future—are marginalized, canceled, and subsumed within the dominant vision and contradictions, and "minority" or "marginal" persons, positions, and ideas are subsumed, dismissed, or otherwise qualified. "Mediation" is understood as the term for the management of beings according to the prevailing dominant ideas or concepts of technologies, logic, and thought of being. Within an historicist understanding, such mediation might be seen as "progress."

Hegelian dialectics very well models the relationship of self to identity on the Internet today. The cultural categories are those that are informative and communicative—informative and communicative language, for example. The social norms are information and communication as clear and distinct statements. And the historicity and logic through which documentary being appears is that of the documentary/information age as mediated by computational technologies using data processing (and sometimes older, documentary tools and techniques) toward document formation and management, with language being understood as an instrumental tool for information transfer and communication. Seen globally, the appearance of personal identities and documentary identities in social computing are moments in the working out of the cultural psychologies and sociologies that are embedded in these systems in the form of algorithms of need (Thomas 2012). These identities are psychological and sociological "facts," indicative of the empirical claims of governing political economies.

The expansion of the logic of citation, from the academic to the more general social sphere, has been accomplished by search and social network algorithms and indexes, which give coherence to vast and arguably fragmented social worlds through a logic of information needs. Needs are fulfilled through algorithms and indexes that construct and link information according to needs that are predicated as attributes of subjects. Such subjects are less that of being selves of hypothetical potentialities, and more persons of logical possibilities (and so, as conforming to such logical norms of expression, they are sometimes seen as objects). As the dialectic historically develops or "matures," such objectivized "personhood" (as the self-conscious concept of being) is introjected into selves at earlier and earlier developmental ages. The curtailment or re-inscriptions of the subject's fantasy to the economy of online systems is a function of not just the personal time and labor, but also the social time and labor, invested through those systems.

Sociocultural Indexes and Computational Algorithms

Ostensibly, with "post-documental" information we do not start with the organization of documents, but with the organization of a person's needs, as identified and organized by user vocabulary and indexed by technical algorithms based on assumed social and semantic relationships and preferences. The semantic web, recommendation systems, Google PageRank, and so forth, are based on the assumption that individual queries are, essentially, social queries, and so can be semantically or socially derived and positioned. From this, persons are connected to named documents and other identities in explicitly or implicitly presented networks. Here we arrive at a certain documental / post-documental historical moment of the modern documentary tradition, where and when documents and other informational substances are no longer largely delivered through explicit professional organizations and standards, but rather are assembled through implicit technical and assumed social codes. These include user terms; network, physical, and social locations and relationships; semantic relationships; and search histories, among others, that bear with them what was once known simply as "the user," who now comes online to be reconstructed in the *figure* of a person, as an intentional and responsible agent, increasingly through a documentary form other than the written text (photographs, avatars, documentary traces, and increasingly, biometric identifiers).

This figure (*figura*) in itself, as a documentary presence or documentary "typology" (Auerbach 1957), is taken as signifying or indexing not only its predicates and other entity relations from these in social and documentation networks, but also as I will discuss in later chapters, through these networks of big data in which they are embedded, such *figura* foreshadow future activities, future figures for the person or the text within the domain of what is, really, automated documentary exegesis.[3]

What we think to be personal intentions—our "needs"—are socially structured through implicit or explicit social computing environments as information and communication needs. We navigate through information and communication technologies, which treat and shape our needs as documented sociocultural identities, tastes, and styles.

What, then, are the mechanisms of power for these new sociocultural indexes? There are, of course, the computational algorithms of social computing technologies. But these must work in dialectical relation with cultural and social norms, from user vocabulary to the user's choices and grammars of vocabulary and social associations. Between the computational algorithms and their social psychological assumptions on the one hand, and the ideological mechanisms that positions persons as social subjects, on the other, there emerges the new type of "user," a product of documentary meaning, identity, and intention. And increasingly today this user is co-positioned with documents and documentary fragments as themselves being documentary units for further reuse. Documentary fragments, here, are like the fragments of medieval religious cosmology: indexical pointings to other representations of persons in the logical space of documents (Walsh 2012; Drucker 2013).[4]

The bridge, then, between the documentation and the information moments of the modern documentary tradition is the concept of need, as needs are shaped by technical practices and their particular modes of positing knowledge and persons as evidence or aboutness (i.e., "information"). A critical theory of this documentary/"information" tradition would have to focus not only upon mediating technologies, but also upon their recursive and historically accumulative functions in the building up of sociocultural indexes.

Indexes of Social Positioning: Style, Taste, and Ideology

Computer-mediated indexes are sociocultural indexes. They construct indexes of sociocultural phenomena through language analyses and through network, physical, and social location analyses, and in recursive systems they then reinvest those indexes into mediating further searching. The result is a dynamic system of self-positioning and social repositioning, where, as Neal Thomas has written, a "dynamic resembling a flock of birds" occurs, for which the movement of each redirects the whole and the whole redirects each (Thomas 2012): what is popularly called a "swarm" or "crowd" dynamic. What newer, internet, information systems represent and re-index back into the search and back into language more generally are not sociocultural forms determined by a professional body (as with older documentary indexing), but rather, the system's representations of the actions and identities of documentary subjects and objects in time as evidence of their "aboutness."

However, what are often not apparent to ordinary users in such systems are the algorithmic infrastructures that mediate the transitions from singularities to individuals—from, for example, my searching on Amazon to its algorithmic recommendations for "Ron." Nor (as I will discuss further in chapter 5) do users often fully know, understand, or appreciate the manners by which users' needs become capital that is invested and reinvested by the owners of the information system into other information and communication systems. Last, recursive social computing systems socially position subjects within new identities by gathering up users and documents together into user groups and communicational forums and strengthening existing sociocultural tastes, styles, and ideologies, which can sometimes result in very productive environments and yet other times in rich, but isolated and narrowing, islands of language and being. This "displacing energy" of "the flock" in social networks (Thomas 2012) can also be described as the dialectic of personal and group needs.

We are aware of the dominant technical functions of some of the more popular social computing systems: Google's PageRank characterized by a link-analysis system of indexing and ranking, Amazon's recommendation system, and Facebook's indexing of semantic, social, and physical network relationships.

However, there has been little discussion of the other side of the dialectic, the sociocultural functions. Technical algorithms dialectically work with sociocultural horizons to form historically specific, dynamic indexes of normative social and cultural spaces. How do social computing systems incorporate "user preferences" at the most ineffable reaches of personal choice and social positioning? Vocabulary alone tells us very little about social positioning when it occurs beyond tightly structured domains. As has long been understood in information science, we need understandings of linguistic syntaxes (derived through grammatical, discursive, and rhetorical analysis, or through semantic inference) and social syntaxes (derived through URLs, IP addresses, social relationships on the net or derived through social network analyses) in order to gain more predictive indexes of future needs based on what a person is assumed to do as a part of personal, social, and cultural "trends."

Cultural and social analyses in modernity have referred to these larger sociocultural parameters for individual and group social positioning according to terms such as "taste," "style," and "ideology." The first two terms belong to the domain of aesthetics. Taste refers to subjective judgments of harmony or disharmony that lead to group inclusion or exclusion. One has judgments of taste regarding objects, people, or events, liking them or not, finding them beautiful or not, and so forth, but such judgments conform or not to other people's tastes, as well. Tastes are emotional judgments that socially position the self in regard to others.

Style refers to the particular way a thing is done—to an aesthetic syntax or rhythm. It, too, is aesthetic, in the sense that, in Kant's language, there is not a matching and subordination of the object or event to categories of understanding, but rather, a judgment is made of style in relation to one's likes or dislikes. One likes someone's style or not, this is the newest style in a designer's fashion line, one has one's own style (distinct from others), and so on.

Read from the viewpoint of aesthetics, ideological judgments are aesthetic in the sense that they are emotive, "unconscious" acts of self-positioning within social, cultural, and overall political norms. Human beings are highly social animals, and their use of relatively sophisticated language and other semantic sign systems as communicational means allows persons to be social even when in relative physical isolation. (When left in isolation or dreaming, people *must* talk to themselves.) Ideology is the *logos* or the arrangement of ideas or concepts. Ideology is the arrangement of conceptual forms that make the world as a whole—to borrow a term from Heidegger (1962), *zuhanden*, or ready-to-hand—graspable as a concept. "Information" and its "society" and "age" are graspable as a concept of the world most by those who live within the social benefits of its technologies and their tropes, but also by those who are forced to, either from necessity or from hope. This is always the way it is with ideology, and why it really is so readily recognizable. It forms the totality of what Heidegger called the "ontic"—the commonsense everyday or "folkloric" way in which we look at the world *as the world*.

In Marxist discourse, ideology is seen as holding together real relations in a mode of capitalist production. Through ideology we understand what is and the way it is according to some coherent (or at least we suppose coherent) vision of the world, which overcomes all the paradoxes of how things occur. Within ideology, conceptual or discursive positions, statements of fact, opinion, and explanations for actions are expressed by the self without critical consideration upon the social, cultural, and political construction of these expressions. When understood through Kant's notion of the aesthetic, the self through ideology feels comfortable with itself in its world because his or her utterances fit within a rational mode of understanding by others.

The inscriptions of the self in aesthetic judgments (in the Kantian sense)— unconscious prejudgments or what we today call "prejudices"— often take place at the point of linguistic and social syntaxes, rather than individual words (though, of course, individual words may become "power words" in situations that mobilize larger sets of actions and words). We can tell someone's tastes and style and we can read their actions as ideological only if we see them express themselves in an extended syntax of words and actions over time and such conform to (categorical) "class" biases. When we experience others saying or doing something in the same or like way over time, then we make judgments based on the form, rather than dominantly the content, of their words and actions. Such judgments are made via recognition from past experiences, and so they are in this sense aesthetic in nature. We feel that these others and their expressions are *like* or not, and so, as we say in English, we often *like* them or not, based on this. "Liking," here, is a mode of being at home with others based on feelings of similar judgments. It is the way of identifying with someone through shared predications.

From these forms, we then make predicative judgments for an identity and, if it is a person, his or her intentions. Viewed critically, so-and-so acts in such a way, despite the logic of the situation, and so we say that he or she demonstrates an ideological bias, especially if the context is recognized as being "class based" (which is often understood as an economic class). So-and-so demonstrates a liking for impressionist, rather than expressionist, painting, and so has a particular taste in art (and so, crudely, we may like or dislike them or their judgments based on this). So-and-so has certain ways of doing certain things and so he or she demonstrates a style in approaching certain types of problems or everyday affairs. And so, too, texts exhibit certain points of view by their narrative consistency and genre forms; they have their unique styles that we attribute to an author (high cultural forms) or a genre (low cultural forms). Texts belong to certain social categories and appeal to high and low tastes by their diction. And they exhibit certain authorial styles in their grammatical and rhetorical syntaxes.

From a computational perspective, it is the job of software algorithms and indexing to sort out these qualities and to help orient a person toward such groupings or to exclude them from a personal search. The documentary user is being reborn as a subject of social computing systems.

Interpellation

These terms—*taste, style,* and *ideology*—are very important for our analysis of information systems because they indicate how both persons and documents are mediated by not only the technologies and rules of computational algorithms, but also by the rules of sociocultural norms.

Within documentary systems, persons and texts are positioned through documentary algorithms and indexes. The sociotechnical positioning of subjects within groups and of groups within subjective responses and needs may be characterized psychologically and politically by the function of "interpellation," and in terms of the mathematical functions of social computing algorithms by its near homonym, "interpolation."

Let us start with the issue of ideology. For the French Marxist Louis Althusser (who was influenced by the psychoanalyst Jacques Lacan's understanding of subjectivity as being constructed through symbolic fields), "interpellation," from "*interpeller*" (meaning to call out, to hail, to heckle), involves the subject coming to understand him- or herself as a subject of reference in response to a particular type of hailing or call (Althusser 2001). From the point of view of Lacan's "algebraic" formulations, as well as social computing algorithms, the subject is viewed as a subject by virtue of its social positioning within an economy of language and other semantic references. The subject, and subjectivity, is viewed as being a social *function.*

One of the primary goals of undergoing clinical psychoanalysis is to arrive at the point of being a functioning subject through an understanding of one's place in the world. This social positioning is precisely the point of critique in Althusser's critical remarks about the subject's position within ideology. From a Marxist viewpoint, subjects in capitalism are positioned through their psychological and social development, and through continual discipline and coding, to reproduce the labor and values that are important to capital. The person is thus not only called upon, but also through algorithmic systems their future actions are predicted, through interpolations based on past performances and social norms. These predictive points then are reinforced by advertising or other means so that the subject comes increasingly to view his- or herself according to likely future interpolations with less and less deviancy at each point. This is exactly the type of self-estimation and self-shaping that is required of persons in systems that demand maximum performance. Learning and human development are integral for creating the conditions for interpellation, and it is into learning and human development that algorithms and indexes are most effectively placed for determining a documentary spirit and establishing a documentary means of governance and self-governance. Self-commodification and a transformation of personal singularity to an estimated ideal most successfully occurs when introjected into the subject as an ego-ideal, which developmentally guides the acquisition of knowledge and modes of expression. In psychoanalytic discourse, "introjection" refers to the mental coding of the subject by cultural forms and social norms, forming unconscious systems of semantic forms and of rules and roles for expression.

In his late essay, "Ideology and the Ideological State Apparatus," Althusser (2001) illustrates the manner by which persons come to recognize themselves as subjects through calls from an authoritative law that address him or her as a "me" within a moral and political order. This "me," this object pronoun, becomes the ego-ideal form for the "I," the subject pronoun, which grammatically marks the intentional human agent.

The call seems to come out of nowhere, because it is the voice of conscience (the call of the superego or *das Über-Ich*); it is the voice of an external authority that has been given the power to construct and curb desire (the id or *das Es*) and create the ego (the I or *das Ich*)—less as a self and more as a person within moral (and for Althusser, primarily economic and political) orders. In Althusser's conceptualization of interpellation, following Lacan's work, the Freudian topology of the id, ego, and superego is understood within a linguistic, and particularly, a communicational framework, but one in which the individual is literally in-formed as a subject by the performance and affect of the call, even before its particular content.

One is interpellated into line, or literally, *ordered* within a moral and political regime, by this call, which is backed by indoctrinations into the state's righteousness and force.

This is Althusser's famous example of the interpellation of the ideological subject:

As a first formulation I shall say: all ideology hails or interpellates concrete individuals as concrete subjects, by the functioning of the category of the subject.

This is a proposition which entails that we distinguish for the moment between concrete individuals on the one hand and concrete subjects on the other, although at this level concrete subjects only exist insofar as they are supported by a concrete individual.

I shall then suggest that ideology "acts" or "functions" in such a way that it "recruits" subjects among the individuals (it recruits them all), or "transforms" the individuals into subjects (it transforms them all) by that very precise operation which I have called interpellation or hailing, and which can be imagined along the lines of the most commonplace everyday police (or other) hailing: "Hey, you there!"

Assuming that the theoretical scene I have imagined takes place in the street, the hailed individual will turn round. By this mere one-hundred-and-eighty-degree physical conversion, he becomes a subject. Why? Because he has recognized that the hail was "really" addressed to him, and that "it was really him who was hailed" (and not someone else). Experience shows that the practical telecommunication of hailings is such that they hardly ever miss their man: verbal call or whistle, the one hailed always recognizes that it is really him who is being hailed. And yet it is a strange phenomenon, and one which cannot be explained solely by "guilt feelings", despite the large numbers who "have something on their consciences." (Althusser 2001, 117–118)

Althusser's example is of a policeman hailing a person, but this constitutes for Althusser an "operation" or "function"— a set of technologies and techniques—within a telecommunicational situation. Why "telecommunication"? First, because the call comes from a distance ("hail"); second, because it involves a short, distinct, operation of message transmission; and third, because the distance that it is transmitted across is not just a physical distance, but a psychological one: the person is taken out of his or her selfhood and transported into being a person within a public order. And last, because in true statistical fashion for information message signaling (as in Claude Shannon's model) it involves the averaging and estimating of value for the individual based on statistical norms. The individual is predicated as a subject by social psychology and law in the operation of the call, and this call is then taken up or "received" by the subject because it is understood as the voice of law through the psychological and moral makeup of the individual as a subject. In other words, *informational communication occurs because the dialectical positions of the caller and the respondent are part of a logic of understanding, communication, and conscience that has been introjected into individuals through learning and experience, cultural institutions, and sometimes by threat of force. Subjects* are, literally, *evidence* of a socio-cultural-technical system, which constitutes for them a subjectivity, that is, a function or *way* of being; a system to which they respond by their very performances and expressions. It is to the subject position within the call that the individual responds. The call belongs not solely to either the policeman or to the one being called by the policeman. Such a call belongs, first of all, to a discursive order of the law (legal, moral, and social). It is one way that we belong to a social order and it is an important way for us to be recognized and to have value for another and ourselves as social animals. For this reason, the individual responds to the policeman's call, and the policeman is responding to a more abstract and general moral and political call of the law, as well.

Subjects are beings who belong to moral orders. To be a subject, and so to be treated as one who has and takes on *respons*ibilities (that is, abilities or skills in responding), one *must* first of all have incorporated the unconscious skill, the habit, of responding to a call. In modernity, to respond to a call is, first of all and above all, to be able to respond to the anonymity of the call, an anonymity that comes from sociocultural, state, and institutional systems (e.g., the legal system) to which both the caller and the called respond in the form of expressions and practices. The foundational calls of modern institutions appear as anonymous as they summon consumers and producers, victims and persecutors, subjects and objects into a common space of responding to one another, all held together by the more primary moral and political requirement of responding to the call of the logic of the system itself as a sanctified, normative, *way of being*. For better or worse, such ways answer the question of being in not only a comforting manner, but also an acceptable manner, for the social being that human beings are. They give to individuals a meaning and a sense, literally beyond their own singular particularities. (Though these moral orders may still conflict with one another and have to be resolved in ethical decisions by individuals within situations of what Derrida termed "undecidability.")

Telephonics is an early technological example of our moral training of responding to calls that far precedes and extends beyond the technology of the telephone, lying in the techniques, logics, and grammars of social and cultural responding and self-positioning. One answers calls in certain ways; this is the most fundamental training of any child as a responsible child—responding to others, whether via the telephone or some other technology. The developmental extension of one's response to a call—from the formation of a social and cultural conscience to a moral conscience to a technological conscience—is a phenomenon that also lies at the heart of information and communication technologies' abilities to both answer needs and also extend those needs by their own sociotechnical devices. The call behind interpellation, namely, the call of subjectivity itself, is why we can't put the phone down and why the Internet keeps us hanging on, often addictively. (As Avital Ronell has argued in her works, addiction is, essentially, an issue of the sublimation of *Mitsein*.) This is, at heart, the source of what we might call the psychotechnical pathologies that define a "digital culture" or "digital society," and so, a "digital being," and which, indeed, make many other important modern technologies indispensible.[5] There is an originary ontic concept or idea to needs, an inscription to desire, a logic and grammar of rational organization and action upon being, which ideology supports. With each movement of the dialectic, it both reasserts itself practically and retreats further back into the obscurity of not being seen as a purely theoretical concept. Far from being seen in the moment of Hegelian absolute being, a concept of being disappears from obvious view while each of the beings embody and show it—"empirically" as this term is used in the social sciences—giving way to a higher level of subsumption and a greater level of embodiment. The core of an episteme disappears in its very fulfillment, dwelling in a subsequent concept that expresses the former one in a comparatively new form. In such a way, the "secret" of a concept of being is passed on from one generation of technology and subjects to another. A "culture" and a "tradition" are formed, as metaphysical continuities, generation after generation.

In a footnote to the above quoted section of his essay, Althusser notes that the interpellation he refers to is a very specific type of hailing, namely a policeman hailing an individual as a suspect in a crime. The individual is the "one" that is hailed. As a suspect in a crime one must respond to a charge; this charge is not only in the content of the address, but first of all in its tone—that is what makes it a *charge* and not just an inquiry. There is a total economy of language, society, and a way of being that one is responding to, not just to an individual person. One is called forth within an evidentiary system in order to *represent* oneself as *fully present* in the here and now. One must present all that one has been and is in a way that satisfies the system. One must intuitively understand its logic (or hire a legal representative who understands it). One must understand the types of subjects that it calls out to and demands evidence of, and the averages that it assumes, the leveling out of data points in one's life. In brief one must *document* one's self as innocent or otherwise.

It is a sociocultural, technological, modern documentary system that is calling one, as one. The moral demand of this interpellation upon a person is that one understands the nature of evidence and what is being asked for. First of all, it demands that one has formed a notion of the documented subject within one's self, before the internalized voice of, say, the legal system and its institutions, so that one knows how to respond in the actual situation of presenting one's self before the law when the moment comes when one is called upon to do so.

Being hailed, one must understand dialectic in a particular sociocultural and political order. One must have internalized the law of the subject *before* the call of the law or any other moral order. One must be prefigured to receive the hail of the order *as a subject in a documentary way*, otherwise, one cannot represent one's self either well or adequately, and may not even know enough to respond. (Failure in this last will result in the greatest force of discipline and punishment being exerted upon one, because it is, beyond all else, *the* moral-political error not to be able to document one's self within a modern institutional order in the way called for; a fundamental error of a lack of social maturity which requires a primitive and *unforgettable* means of punishment. One *must* know enough, if anything, to respond to the call of a system, to be responsible as an identity in whatever is understood as an organized system, otherwise, one cannot subsequently defend one's self and, therefore, one cannot be either guilty or not guilty as charged. One is first of all, as Kafka put it in the title of his story, "Before the Law"—"Vor dem Gesetz.")

Let us stress that in Althusser's example, the policeman is looking for *evidence*, namely, evidence that one is a certain type of person or not. He or she is looking for one to represent one's self in terms of the interpellation that one is brought within, as being either true or false to that type. One is being called to document one's self as a being that fits (or does not) an information need, as determined by a system of documents of suspicion. An individual is called into such a system, as "one," within a typology of documentary signs.

But, again, before that particular investigation, there exists an already general system of representation to which one responds as "naturally" belonging to. In modernity, one belongs to a documentary society, a society in which one's being *is* in so much as it is evidenced, *proved* (what Avital Ronell referred to as "the test drive" [Ronell 2005], a tendency exacerbated by the neoliberalist virtue of competition). One must prove one's self within systems of proof or evidence; this is the political and moral economy of life's meaning—of one's being—in such systems.

One is pre-enrolled as a subject upon birth, and then within a range of types of subjective being. This pre-enrollment takes place from birth onward, when physical needs are answered by cultural and social inscriptions, which transform those self-needs into person-needs, with the resulting transformation of the self-who-needs into a subject-who-knows-how-to-respond, and so knows how to articulate his or her needs in the language of dominant reality and its symbolic orders (that is, the transformation into a subject who now needs information or knowledge). In this sense, above all, ideological calls are "telecommunication" because the practice of communication—and the practice of the dialogical inscription of subjects as information needs (and as responding to those needs)—occurs *within* the inscription of a prior opening. The logic of the communication that forms the hail—that of call and response, of information need and documentary evidence—takes place within an arrangement of understandings whereby the self has come to understand itself as a person within orders of recognition and evidence. The logic of communication takes place within a documentary logic, which structures the self as a *responsible* subject that *responds* not simply to an other, but first of all to the symbolic order itself and its logic of identity and expression in terms of the presenting of evidence.

In social computing algorithms relationships are based on logical inference or interpolated proximity. Relevancy in information retrieval is suggested to the subject as a statistical relation. One becomes, *pace* Briet (2006), an indexical sign by one's inclusion as evidence within a taxonomy of likely types ("initial documentation") and, further, within discursive systems that link one's identity to other documents ("secondary documentation"). The self becomes a document, both to others and to one's own present, past, and futures (through recursive systems), and through their indexes the documents become agents who shape the searchers' past, present, and future being.

Who calls to me through social computing mechanisms? In one sense, obviously, I am being called by the indexes of the algorithms. For example, with Amazon's recommendation system which calls out to me: "Hello, Ron," and then makes recommendations based on my past browsing and buying histories and that of others that it has identified to be like me. Here, I am being hailed as one suspected of being interested in some thing or another. I can also set up in "push" technologies or recommendation systems fields of documentary indexes to hail me as someone interested in various things. Facebook hails me as someone likely to be interested in other people who know people that I know. Simply by having an identity online we are now hailed by other people. And we are first of all hailed by the sociotechnical information system itself (as representative and mediator of a political economy) as a fulfiller of an information need. We come to hail ourselves as certain representations of persons by our very searching and communicating online.

In Internet social computing systems, the commodification of identity becomes very difficult for the user to control. One is caught up in past selves that one may no longer wish to be; one is caught up by what others think and whom others know; one must manage many different social systems (e.g., scholarly identity, personal identity, local community identity, credit identity, popular cultural identity). In short, if one is to try and present one's self wholly consistently, one must try and become a corporation or conglomeration of one's different selves, unified into a brand. One must devote time and budget to building and maintaining this brand. Managing the systems that discuss and process one's identity can become complex, as one can be assessed from many points of view, in many different networks. One can be interpellated and interrogated in so many various ways. Every person with access to a computer and an Internet connection now has the possibility of being a media(ted) star.

What Althusser (2001) is calling interpellation is a two-fold process. First, there is the displacement of the personal psychological self (understood as a toolbox of hypothetical *potentials*) by a social psychological person (as a set of logical *possibilities* within a discursive or symbolic order). And second, there is the psychological introjection of that figure into the individual in the mode of an expressive subject—that is, in the mode of expressive forms, styles, and tastes that correspond to needs that can be satisfied within a political economy. Here, then, the satisfaction of needs corresponds to a useful and adequate social information system, and individuals as users correspond to queries that can be entered into a social search. In an ideal information system, the system continually readjusts so as to maintain equilibrium of norms for meaning between these two points, resulting in what we call "communication" and "information." *Information* and *communication* mean, here, the stating and satisfying of needs by documents and other people in a system. These demand a stabilization of vocabulary as a prerequisite for language acts, and social computing does this through mediating individual user searches through past searches and group activities and ontologies, and by readjusting the social order based on new user searches. The system moves in an *Aufhebung* of gathering up the subject's needs (expressed through vocabulary, links, etc.) toward the others, reweighting the others' values for the subject's needs, and recalibrating the dialectic as a whole as a moment of progress in the refinement of information for all; Thomas's "flock of birds" where leaders take turns from one another (Thomas 2012a) in satisfying a need.

Social computing modifies the form of human historicity. First, like much of computational space, acts cannot be rewritten except by further acts that modify their weighted values. Similarly, second, acts cannot be, or they resist being, forgotten both in whole and in parts (Blanchette and Johnson 2002). Third, the progress or *Aufhebung* of the system speeds up the overall temporality of the system and its participants. The "new rhythm" (Briet 2006) of a technology introduces a new rhythm in the technicity of human performance. By narrowing options and the formal nature of needs, which increases the speed of information and communication in a system, efficiency is achieved and labor saved. This labor then can be devoted to other tasks, not only over time, but also through the switching in and out of tasks (i.e., multitasking).

The overall limits to the speed of a sociotechnical information and communication system must include the overall goals, tasks, and limits of the person or persons involved. Some, such as Franco Berardi (2001), have suggested that, with the heavy use of networked information and communication technologies, anxiety and depression occur in individuals through the constant switching in and out of cognitive foci with multitasking and the breaking of relations of deep solicitude and their replacement by a temporality of screen attention. As human beings attempt to keep up with the speed of automated systems the nature of psychological temporality changes. This is a constant point of critique for philosophical and critical work in modernity (e.g., the work of the Romantic poets and philosophers of the nineteenth century, and twentieth century critics such as Heidegger, Benjamin, and Habermas), as well as more recent ethnographically based works (e.g., Turkle 2011). Charlie Chaplin's *Modern Times* may have a contemporary equivalent in digital overload.

Indexing It All

Computational social interpellation takes place in symbolic fields, through sociocultural and technical dialectical algorithms that gather up, sublimate, and exclude and include persons and texts toward the formation of users and documents, information needs and information, and increasingly collocated data. Both the expanse of materials and the refinement of information are seen as goals for increasing relevancy for system users. Both have been achieved through the greater availability of documents in digital form for the Internet (or other digital systems), advances in harvesting and indexing the contents of documents, increases in the mediums that collect, harvest, and index the Internet, and not least of all, a greater penetration of interfaces that allow access and searching of these materials. Communication mediums, such as Facebook, work on information indexing and retrieval principles, though with somewhat different ends (more extended flows of information between subjects, rather than temporary or terminal searches; relevancy searches across social networks, etc.).

Let us now briefly return to consider problems of affect—taste and style— as elements in social positioning. For affect is one of the newest horizons for responding to and predicting information (and commodity) needs, and as we will see in the next chapter it is a crucial problem in android design.

Generally, vocabulary itself is not contextual enough to indicate or guide social positioning—we rely on linguistic and sociocultural grammars (in Wittgenstein's sense of "grammar") of language use in order to see which way an inquiry, discourse, or argument is "going." That is, in Frege's language, to see not only the reference or "meaning" of a term, but also its "sense" (Frege 1952; Deleuze 1990). Taste and style, along with ideology, have been critical cultural terms by which we attempt to understand the present-future grammar of a subject. They exist as "feelings" that often ground a subject's further judgments, understanding, and actions. Thus, they are very useful for prediction.

The recognition of a person's style and taste are everyday aesthetic means for inferring present and future social positioning. On the other hand, they are "fuzzy" variables, whose values are derived by observing or recording repeated acts and by social context. One's tastes and styles are shown over time and in relation to others. They are emotive, rather than cognitive, acts, because affective sense is determinate for their meaning. It is therefore not surprising that social networking systems, such as Twitter or Facebook, as well as older markets (such as the stock market), are viewed as sites where taste and style may be investigated and data gathered. In such symbolic markets, taste and style are translated into social value and can achieve communicational contagion. These mass movements then can lead to the reweighting of indexes of value (documentary worth, financial worth). Documents achieve real world sense and popular value by being communicated, not simply by being retrieved. And it is through communication that search engines and documentary indexes most fully become social media, and that the evidence of documents becomes or reinforces norms, ideologies, tastes, and styles.

"Taste" is the term given since the eighteenth century to aesthetic judgments, but in Kant's sense of the term (Kant 2000), judgments of taste were not exclusive to judgments on fine art. Rather, as was remarked earlier, aesthetic judgments more generally—that is, judgments regarding form—align persons with other persons based on their likes and dislikes. From this perspective, together with notions of style, the categories of taste and style bridge personal and social psychologies and act as ineffable indexes of sociocultural class membership for individuals. Today, one important function for social computing software is to anticipate judgments regarding information sources or potential information and communication sources. Taste and style are some of the genres of judgment that social computing attempts to find in syntaxes of language and social and cultural membership vis-à-vis language and other signifying means.

As Althusser's notion of ideology indicates, ideological interpellation is a largely unconscious form of class inscription and expression, through which meaning takes place through a subject and for other subjects. Taste makes up much of the form of ideology and class inclusion in consumer culture. One expresses statements of likes and dislikes regarding commodity items and other people and events, and so aligns one's own person with others through such tokens. In consumer culture, one also expresses a style through objects. Commodity objects offer evidence of one's belonging to a field of taste, style, and use (whether the object is actually used or is just collected); they document a relationship between people in terms of interest domains (knowledge, sports, fashion, idiosyncrasies, etc.). The Internet has been a great boom in erasing the difference between individual traits and social inscription.

Are one's tastes and styles one's own, as it were, or are one's tastes taken directly from some group or "class" taste (*to be* a member of high society, *to be* a punk rocker, *to be* a Harley Davidson motorcycle rider, or *to be* a "redneck")? Here, one is both being something and always striving to be that by maintaining styles of expression. So correspondingly, it may be asked if one's style is made up of unique performative traits or is one "stylistic"—in the sense of "fashionable"—that is, one's "own" style belongs to certain fashions? There are large intercultural and intersocial variances, too, for the moral understanding and evaluation of a person acting at either range of the meaning of "style," with some societies valuing "individual style" and others valuing group belonging. (Though, it is difficult to tell when an individual style is not a group characteristic. For example, is the "individual" style typical in the United States what one means by "individual" in distinction from group belonging [i.e., when it is so typical], or, conversely, is the singular difference in the midst of group conformity, as in Japanese cultural psychology for example, more representative of individuality?)

The semantic horizons of sociocultural genres such as style, taste, and to a more critical sensibility, ideology, mark zones for the merging of personal and social psychologies. Thus, these genres are rich areas for social computing research and design, which attempt to locate individuals as both individuals and as members of groups. Correspondingly, social computing indexes act as computational mediators of personal and group psychology according to affective operations such as "liking" or "disliking" common objects or events, whether they be high or low cultural or social items. Before the Internet, it was easier to take taste and style as one's own. Now, even one's name can no longer be taken as strictly one's own.

In neoliberalism, one must create a market out of one's self. This requires self-positioning, which necessitates seeing one's self from the marketplace eyes of others, as a person within a market of competing goods (and persons being marketplace goods as well). In a digital marketplace one must turn one's self into a marketable person and one's marketable person must take the form of being a documentary and informational commodity; a uniqueness that fulfills an information need, which, however, is not so unique as not to be part of a market. At the same time as it shows our uniqueness, the Internet demands our interpellation/interpolation as an online identity. After all, who, today, wants one's social network "friends" to "dislike" or "de-friend" one? More generally, who doesn't want to be a document for another's need? (There seems to be a sort of adolescent psychological drive operating through these systems.) In the chapter on social big data, we will return to this intersection of the modern documentary tradition and neoliberalism more fully.

In the next chapter, however, we will examine the modern documentary tradition in another epistemic-historical moment, namely in the mimicry of human subjectivity by robot design and the creation and the recursive reinvestment of communicative documents between humans and robots. If persons have become documents for information systems, the desire of android robotics is to make robots (whose actions appear through documents of code) more human. For this to occur information must be turned into communication, or at least some semblance of communication.

5 The Document as the Subject: Androids

"Homo documentator" must prepare himself to take command—with all his senses awake—over the robots of tomorrow. The value of the machine will be that of a servant. "Our ability to overtake machinism lies in our possibilities of assimilating the machine" (Mumford).
—Suzanne Briet, *What Is Documentation?* (1951/2006)

The statement above from Suzanne Briet's book raises the issue of taking command of machines by assimilating them. In this process "man" performs this assimilation in order not to become a mechanism of the machine. As we have seen so far, though, this is tricky because information and communication techniques and technologies increasingly mediate our own understanding of the world, including what such technologies are, within the modern documentary episteme. Machinism is not something that one can simply put at a distance, since *techne* inhabits the type of being that human being is, and modern technologies constitute much of the infrastructures of most people's worlds today. Moreover, information and communication technologies require an infrastructural enfolding of *techne*, so that we forget its very presence in transparency. This transparency often involves a double bind, a "yes" and a "no," to the question of whether the technology mediates or changes information and communication. Even with the telephone, we know that "reaching out to touch someone" (as the old Bell Telephone ads put it) through the telephone reasserts the distance between the two communicators. In the same way, more recently, we see that our online friends come with the caveat of the loss of their not being here, often with the effect of reducing correspondence to mere chitchat. This is the "catch" of all modern information and communication technologies. It is, however, a catch that Plato, too, noted in *Phaedrus* about the technology of writing more generally, understood as a representation of the speaker him- or herself; in other words, writing as a documentary practice. Humans *assimilate* themselves to the technologies, but then these technologies shape not only further technologies, but the very nature of human being itself through their infrastructural, psychological, and, increasingly, physiological incorporation into the human environment and body.

The machine often shows its materiality most when it is explicitly made to be like us. The dream remains to make objects that not only leverage our knowledge, not only document certain aspects of our being and expression, but that are us; machines that we can communicate with, as if to another person. Robots that are not just servants (as per the etymology of the term "robot"), but are also companions—the dream of being living texts, as it were. But further, dialectically, androids are dreamt of as things that assimilate *us* like we assimilate *them* ... a fellow *homo documentator* that is, yet, more than this ... *more human* by being *less* so. Not just a "dumb beast" of a person, nor a mere "parrot" of ourselves either, but something more like us. Android robotics offers an interesting example of Hegel's master-slave dialectic, where the master becomes the slave to the slave by trying to make the latter fit within its mode of a will to power in a certain formation of consciousness.

In this chapter I would like to discuss the problems involved with an android being designed to achieve a psychological being and the limits to which an android can obtain selfhood. With this, I would like to discuss the ways that humans construct their own selves through these robotic others—how humans assimilate themselves to robots in order to (mistakenly or not, consciously or not, successfully or not) "assist" robots in being assimilated to human beings. I would like to further explore the dialectical constitution of being through documentary means, here seen from the view of what we could call "communicative robotics" and "communicative artificial intelligence." These terms describe attempts to build machines whose "intelligence" emerges through their communicative exchanges with people rather than through coding alone. (The modern documentary ontology emerges in all of these: in the coding, in the design of machines as representations of humans, and in the semantic inter-"subjective" space of communicative events that are then taken as documents for further communication.)

Machine learning is an important part of this, but just the beginning. As I will emphasize in this chapter, we must not discount the role of human projection in attributions of machine intelligence nor in facilitating learning by machines. *People become the training sets for their own mimicry*—training sets for both the robots and for the human beings themselves in their relation to the robots. In the dialectical progress of the documentary episteme as a moment in the history of metaphysics, the predicate of "man"—"documentator"—becomes the genus, and the genus becomes the predicate, not through the will of the machines, but through the deployment of the idea in the will of "man." This will expresses itself as power, first of all in the imaginative speculation of the identity of other and self.

Android robotics involves issues of robots being read and being imagined as persons. With androids, "aliveness" means not only linguistic, but also physical responses that pass an android communicative and affective "Turing Test" or standard for thinking that the robotic other is (or at least acts like) a human being. Android robotics—at least understood from the aspect of an engineering project based on *mimesis*—presents the ultimate frontier in the subjectification of the document by having the documentary object physically and emotively appear as a human being. But for this reason, if no other, android robotics presents very interesting issues about how people literally "in-form" one another, not least in subservient relationships, in a certain assertion of the will, where the other is thought of as somewhat less than a self and instead as a malleable subject-object of some sort. (Certain parental, disciplinary, and colonial models, and of course the utilitarian sense of the document-friend that we discussed in the first chapter come to mind here—they all seem to involve, as with pets, a certain domestication, though of a determinate and often violent sort.) As with Heidegger's account of things "ready-to-hand" (Heidegger 1962), where tools are said to show us both their physical presence and their equipmentality most when we no longer use them as a matter of course (when they are broken, for example), it is hoped by some that not only the successes, but also the failures, of android robotics in regard to what I've called the affective Turing Test may show us in part what it is to be human and what it is to be machine.

The purpose of this chapter, then, is not to give a theoretical account of android robotics for the purposes of an engineering project, but rather to account for android robotics as a mode of documentary information-communication; the unfolding and the attempt to fulfill in practice a theory of communication situated within an informational mode and a documentary episteme and model. At the same time, androids produce such a challenge to the mimicry of local and physical human communication that it is dubious that simple formal programs can accomplish the task of overcoming the "uncanny valley." Better models of mind need to be developed and, possibly, bigger data sets need to be made use of in order to arrive at even a practically acceptable expert system, much less one that has physical agency and (even more difficult) physical human characteristics devoid of "uncanny" markers. Indeed, the bar is so high in android robotics because the Turing Test of affective mimicry fails with even the slightest error in appearance, language, or tone of an android robot (unlike, say, a nonhuman-appearing robot or even a humanoid).

Indeed, it is in the fostering of these "productive tones" or "moods," (i.e., other than anxiety or discomfort) that hold us in common, that the android robot fails to "achieve" rather than in the lack of any cognitive achievement. Our being, our *Dasein*, is essentially that of being-with (*Mitsein*); only within this (ontological) being does an (ontic) concept and its logic—a dialectical function or a correspondence model of truth—have any hope (and largely these are just hopes or "models") of functioning. The "uncanny valley" is a mood of anxiety that is created by the dissimilarity of the android, and it is from out of this anxiety that the android fails to deliver or soothe us. If there are to be advances in overcoming the uncanny valley, then overcoming this anxiety and putting in its place moods of solicitude and care is essential.

Within the foundational literature on the "uncanny valley," beginning at least from Masahiro Mori's 1970 article "Bukimi no Tani Genshō" (English translation: Mori 2012), androids are seen as part of a continuum of beings that we psychologically relate to in the modern world. Such beings and things share with us affordances in situations, but they also are understood and shaped by our psychological projections. This demands a psychological understanding based on a dialectical epistemology, and so our psychological examination of androids in this chapter will be based on psychoanalysis, as a psychological framework that stresses the importance of relational development and communication within cultural frames; and within that, specifically, we will use Lacanian psychoanalysis where dialectics plays a very central role in understanding the constitution of self and others, but where, also, Freud's tendencies toward physiological reductionism are curbed and replaced by the importance of social and cultural structures and ideology. (As we will see, historically, psychoanalytic discourse enters into the discourse of android robotics early on, namely in regard to the discourse on the "uncanny valley" between humans and androids.)

Communicative Androids in Cultural and Social Context

Though the generalized claims of cultural psychology are difficult to assess, one of the more striking attributes of Japanese social psychology, in comparison with that of the Western European countries and the Americas, is the rather strong normative categories that people are expected to fit within, both as a self and a person. At the same time, however, the moral boundaries that constitute a self and person seem sometimes to be quite a bit broader than in Western culture. Japanese society is known for socially adjusting to subgroups and behavior that in Western cultures might be considered as needing legal suppression and psychological interdiction.

It is true that it can be quite difficult to operationalize cultural differences, even for descriptive purposes; first because of the hermeneutics of such descriptions, second because any individual occupies cultures and subcultures simultaneously, as well as is a singular assemblage of tools and experiences from these, and third because the boundaries of what constitutes a culture or subculture are rather indeterminate in many instances. However, the adjustment to uncomfortable behaviors as part of the social spectrum (at least within the strictures of what are thought internally to be part of Japanese society or "character") may be read as the other side of the coin of a personal psychology strongly grounded in social psychology, rather than in metaphysical conceptions of the self and individuality.

In beginning this section on android robotics by discussing Japanese cultural psychology, I hope to provide some analogical suggestions as to the direction that personal psychology in the West may be going in the shift from the understanding of the user as being distinct from documents to being inscribed in the logic of the documentary objects that the user uses and understands. I have stressed in the previous chapters that the informational trajectory of the documentary episteme involves the infrastructural inscription of personal "information needs" within sociocultural algorithms. Documentary systems now embed privileged psychological assumptions into the functions of mediating documentary devices and systems, resulting in not only document retrieval, but also in the social construction of friend relationships and the like, as well as online personal identities that correspond to and support these assumptions. In a networked environment, the result may be the emergence of a personal psychology that is more socially mediated, rather than one that is based on the metaphysics of a transcendental ego.

The convergence of Japanese cultural psychology—with its heavy reliance upon categories of social norms for the emergence of personal identity, and yet its valorization of the self within those norms—and android robotics has been noted by several scholars working in android robotics (MacDorman, Vasudevan, and Ho 2009; Šabanović 2010), and so has emerged as one framework through which to try and explain the strong interest in, and acceptance of, androids and social robotics more generally in Japan. But besides being an explanatory framework, this interest in cultural psychology highlights one of the aspects of android robotics that marks a substantial research agenda for the artificial intelligence that drives these robots—that is, a shift from an autonomous view of agency in robotics to a communicational view—that is, a shift from autonomous AI to what we might call "communicative AI."

Since their beginnings robotics and AI have been rooted in an autonomous view in two ways: first, as physically autonomous machines, and second, as formalized documents of program code. As for being physically autonomous machines, robots have tended to be physically distinct as an individual body performing actions. So, for example, "symbiotic" or augmented robotics, such as mechanical exoskeletons (developed for carrying heavy gear over rough terrain in military operations and to help those with missing limbs or paralysis walk or lift heavy objects), have less the sense of being "robots" to the popular imagination than do autonomous designs. As for formalized code, the limits of "traditional AI" epistemologies and techniques of symbol processing have led to more recent emphases upon neural, and other, learning models and architectures for AI "thinking" (Ekbia 2008).

If we want a machine to approach a human ontology (or that of any other higher order animal), it must first of all communicate somewhere in that "higher" order. The traditional fundamental difference between humans and machines has been that humans emerge out of experience and machines emerge out of design. Up until recently, and still largely, machines must be designed and programmed for expression. This difference is at the heart of the uncanny valley between humans and androids and why we expect other beings to be alive when we attempt to communicate with them. To be alive means to show both the versatility and the hesitation that comes with choice and intention, and these develop out of experience. There is a unique rhythm to individual beings, in both what they individually do and what they don't do, that is difficult for a machine to replicate. For this reason, the projection of human needs onto such machines is even more important, for it allows human beings to treat the machine as a body and it forces them to adapt to the machine.

Communication, however, is not just characterized by a hermeneutics of understanding with others and with the environment at large. Communication is also to some degree scripted. With the environment, it is scripted through temporal and spatial continuities and frames of understanding. With other people, and to some degree with other animals, it is scripted through semantic exchanges that form, and are made up of, syntaxes of meaning and sense (Wittgenstein's language games). The degree to which a communicational exchange involves attempts at understanding or involves scripted action varies with the context. The end goal is the same—affect (either physically or ideationally, we want to be *moved* and react to, and do, actions).[1]

In textual and psychological hermeneutics the problem of understanding involves mediating different or conflicting frames for understanding. We may ostensibly see the same things and events, but we bring different assumptions, experiences, and evaluations to those things and events. What is missed from this view, however, is that perspective is not just a problem of frames, but of psychological and textual indexes, and that agreements or not in understanding are indexical problems. A "frame" for understanding or a "perspective" is really nothing other than a *point of view* taken from constellations of signs tied to experience, which are connected to previous signs and experiences. This point of view, coming from a personal index of signs and experiences, represents the gathering together of referential networks that create a unique self, which has been constructed over time. To share a point of view means to share at a certain point in time a referential network that gives a more or less common meaning and/or sense to a thing or event. The contrary applies to not sharing a point of view: I view the U.S. Congress's actions on a legislative bill in a certain way, but you view them in another way. It isn't just that we have different judgmental "glasses" or "frames" on, but rather that we bring different networks of referents, that is, different "experiences" to our personal understanding of a thing or event.

In a sense, though, we might say that though individuals have points of views, it is points of view (as unique constellations of experiences) that have, and indeed make up, individuals. A singular individual is an indexical point, a situated temporal and spatial focus of a person's lifetime of experiences, present awareness, and expectations. A person's mental "inside," as one sometimes says, *is* the set of experientially based tools and potentials that tie together the individual and the environment, folding the "outside" "in" and constituting an individual's past, present, and future. We are like a spider in a web; existing and being present only through the weavings of signifiers that go out in every direction and that connect past and future, with one's self tenuously positioned as present. If we were to cut these webs, then like a ladder that we stand on kicked out beneath us, we would fall into irrationality, as the signifiers that hold us in those Kantian a priori frames of spatial, temporal, and causal continuities lose the indexical historical and sociocultural relationships that keep them strong. The singular individual is built through webs of experience and communication between the constructed individual and the world, resulting in a living, world-positioning index for the individual that is unique in its singularity, but common in its cultural forms, social norms, and sense of bodily extension in space (Day 2007).

Communicative AI attempts to build a subject out of a robot through programming and through experience gained by information exchange and communication. Android robotics attempts to take this further, by extending communication to the affects of bodily presence.

Integral to this project is getting humans to treat robots as communicative and affective agents. The dialectic that is required is not only communicative, but also perceptual and affective. The android must not only look like, but also act like a person in order for the affective-communicational circuit to be complete. This is quite difficult; people are very sensitive to perceptual cues, as well as verbal cues, and especially when these are put together, there can be emotive and cognitive dissonance in interacting with androids. In addition, we seem to still lack a full understanding of how people order cultural forms and social norms, not only in cognitive judgments, but also in moral and aesthetic judgments, and so this presents challenges for even having a competent intelligence component, no matter if such should be embodied in formal programming or gathered through machine learning from large data sets.

The Uncanny Valley

The term for the dissonance that occurs in human activity with androids is the "uncanny valley" (MacDorman and Ishiguro 2006; Mori 2012). Overcoming the uncanny valley between humans and android robots largely entails overcoming a communicative and affective Turing Test.

Masahiro Mori's 1970 article on the uncanny valley of robotic emotive affects upon people, which began the discourse on the uncanny valley, has a diagram (given below) that illustrates such affects:

As Mori's article suggests, androids mark a point on an affective continuum ranging from industrial robots to healthy persons, passing through

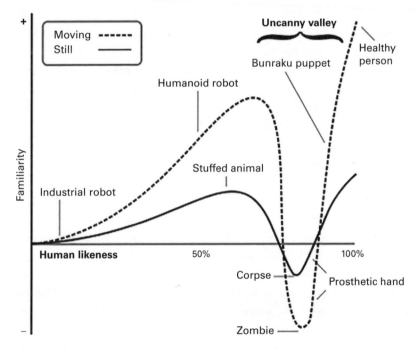

© 2012 IEEE. Reprinted, with permission, from M. Mori (2012), "The Uncanny Valley" (trans. Karl F. MacDorman and Norri Kageki), *IEEE Robotics & Automation Magazine, 19*(2), 98–100.

humanoid robots and stuffed animals and bottoming out with dead bodies and zombies. While Mori's argument has sometimes been treated as an unsupported hypothesis or theory, it may perhaps be better seen as a philosophical description of affective relationships between humans and androids, and as such, empirical testing is neither its point nor is it applicable. Philosophical models are not hypotheses, but rather they are conceptual experiments in our ways of speaking about and understanding things and events.

As Karl MacDorman, who has written extensively and sensitively on the concept of the uncanny valley has pointed out, the term "uncanny" in the original Japanese is *bukimi*, which has the connotations of eerie or strange, in the sense of there being ghosts or phantasms (MacDorman and Ishiguro 2006). Despite this Japanese origin, the literature on the uncanny valley of human-android relations often begins with a psychological discussion of the uncanny in the Western cultural tradition, starting with Sigmund Freud's well-known 1919 essay "Das Unheimliche," translated as "The Uncanny" (Freud 1959). Like many other German-language authors in the nineteenth and early twentieth centuries, Freud used this term to refer to various types of odd and psychologically disturbing phenomenon. It is to this article that we will turn in the hopes of illuminating the phenomenon of the uncanny valley.

Freud's work (1919) cites the earlier 1906 work of the German psychiatrist Ernst Jentsch, "On the Uncanny" (Jentsch 1996), though in his text Freud rejects as overly simplistic Jentsch's conclusion that feelings of the uncanny are due to category errors in cognitive judgments. Both authors focus their central concerns upon automatons, foremost discussing E. T. A. Hoffmann's short story "The Sandman." For both Jentsch and Freud the category error produced by the perceiver's inability to grasp the appearance or actions of the automaton within the concept of "human being," despite the automaton's initial appearances, leads to a feeling of unease in the perceiver. (The intellectual origin for the psychological and the aesthetic epistemology here, seems to be, respectively, Kant's notion of the understanding in his *Critique of Pure Reason* and the feeling of the negative sublime in his *Critique of Judgment*.) In one of many respects, Freud's article differs from Jentsch's in asserting that the experience of the uncanny involves the reassertion of phylogenetic or individual repressed beliefs— "the *unheimlich* is what was once *heimisch*, home-like, familiar; the prefix 'un' is the token of repression" (Freud 1959, 399)—though it needs to be added that "The Uncanny," like many of Freud's other theoretical essays (i.e., those not arising from therapeutic case studies), is not uniform in its conclusions, but exploratory in many directions.

In this last regard, perhaps the more interesting reading of the uncanny that Freud gives, which weaves in and out and concludes his article, runs somewhat parallel to Jentsch's conclusions but develops them in a new direction. Freud's observation at the end of his article is that uncanny phenomena often appear in literary writing, rather than real life, and that they more frequently occur among young children, rather than with adults. Freud's view that the uncanny is an experience in the context of a narrative setting is perhaps a very important clue for understanding the phenomenon of the uncanny valley.

What is important in this observation by Freud, and what in it would "go beyond" (as Freud wished to do) Jentsch's claims that the uncanny is made up of category errors? Why would some event be seen as uncanny in some genres of literature and not in others? Freud states that the uncanny does not occur when reading or hearing fairy tales (which have large degrees of cognitive dissonance with real life), but rather, the uncanny is an experience that occurs when reading more realistic genres, such as is the case with Hoffmann's tale.

Realistic narrative literature is important here because through realistic narratives there occurs a correspondence between the reader's perspective and that of the narrator and the characters. There is a "suspension of disbelief" (Samuel Taylor Coleridge's term) in the very act of reading such a narrative, which requires the reader's identification with the point of view of the narrator—what Coleridge called "poetic faith" (Coleridge 1984). The uncanny feeling is an affective product of the very difference between the realistic setting and the progress of events in the story line. In the case of fairy tales, realism is suspended by our expectations of the genre or from the very start of the narrative by the words, "Once upon a time." But in uncanny stories the overall story frame is realistic, though with significant deviations at key moments in the narrative.

Not surprisingly, as is also the case with almost all horror stories, many of these deviations most often involve the confusion of living and dead things. MacDorman and Ishiguro have linked this confusion to the question of whether what is essential about the uncanny in android robotics is that the not-quite-human android evokes a fear of death in the perceiver (MacDorman and Ishiguro 2006). This would be a position not so far from Freud's (1959), in that the uncanny object would reawaken repressed thoughts of mortality and death. While this is perhaps true, uncanny experiences constitute a wider domain of dissonance between animate and inanimate objects, though the dissonance with human beings may strike us as the most gruesome. Sticks at night being mistaken as snakes, and human part-objects, such as prosthetic limbs, may also elicit uncanny experiences (Mori 2012).

By combining these insights we are led to the conclusion that the uncanny valley appears because of intentional or causally expected actions that are interrupted by their contraries, particularly when the contraries involve ambiguity in the appearance or actions of others, especially humans, in the environment. The context for this, however, are situations that involve what Martin Heidegger (another writer on the *unheimlich*), referred to in *Being and Time* as various forms of care or solicitude (*Sorge, Fürsorge, Besorgen*). Because we identify with a narrative or sympathize with another person, we can be shocked or disturbed by dissonances in what we expect their appearances or actions to be. Humans (and other animals, certainly) have sympathetic relationships with other beings in this world by virtue of their co-occupying the world, and especially when the other appears or acts more like themselves.

Our concern or care for others involves our reading upon the other our own experiences and our anticipations and values of actions performed by an intentional agent. A *projective* understanding—an understanding of others in terms of what we previously understand and anticipate of (and value or not about) them—seems to be fundamental in human relationships, whether the other is empirically present or we try to understand them through produced texts or traces of past actions. Realistic narratives absorb a reader's intentions in the intentions exhibited by the agents of the text and their environments. Currently, achieving this with androids is difficult to do. Androids would need to exhibit not only continuities of action and unities of intention, but human-like vicissitudes within contexts that would show human intention, choice, and that human mode of intended action that is commonly called "will."

The failure to pass an android-human Turing Test and the feeling of the uncanny occur because of the initial assumption that this other *should* act the way I expect a human to act. And if it doesn't act in such a way, then my response will be either pity or worry (is he or she ill?) or if the other acts aggressively or not at all, then, perhaps fear or uncertainty. The uncanny experience is strongest when faced with those robot agents that most resemble humans because of our abilities to perceive the slightest difference in the appearance and behavior of other human beings. As Jentsch, Freud, and Mori all noted, the feeling of the uncanny is a result of an *aesthetic*, as well as a cognitive, judgment. With aesthetics judgments, *pace* Kant, we judge how a thing appears to us; we look at its form and compare it with other forms. As Mori's graph shows, the ontology of affective judgments with androids has a place on a continuum of other affective judgments regarding, especially, humans and human-appearing objects (stuffed animals, dead bodies, zombies, etc.).

Judgments of likeness and dislikeness are based not only on what the other seems to lack, but also on what the other has. Mutlu et al. (2009), for example, have done experiments that use gaze to suggest intentionality. Silence, hesitation, recalcitrance, and seemingly neutral affects in interpersonal interaction all play a role in "absorbing" and "repulsing" individuals into and from each other, just as texts may absorb or frustrate readers. For this reason, as we will soon discuss further, fully scripted interactions are not sufficient to satisfy human communication needs in perhaps the majority of cases of either human role playing or in android-human interactions, save where such is expected (e.g., phone directory services, etc.). There is a crucial moment of response that reveals the integrity and truth of human intentions in any situation, and while this may be masked in part over the short term, over time, as is said in English, the various "true colors" of a person shine through. Individually, one responds to an encounter that has always already been prepared in some general way by our experiences as living beings together. The uniqueness of an expression takes place in a commonality of possible responses. A response to an encounter is given in words or other gestures, and human meaning appears as intentions toward future actions (and will come to characterize the particular being of the individuals involved). It emerges out of an indetermination between what came before and what is present in any encounter.

There are many other problems toward giving robots "souls" that are seen to be humanlike—that is, to give them a presence *not just of mind, but of human being*, which may be enough to suggest personhood, or even beyond this, a selfhood that is physically, emotionally, and cognitively enough *humanlike* as to pass mimetic tests. Just two examples are those of rhythms and modulations in pace and tone of voice, and a person's ability to manipulate social situations as tools for making the environment suitable (Cowley and MacDorman 2006).

Indeed, in order to manage the problem of the complexity of human intersubjective affects as a barrier to human-robot interaction, as Šabanović (2010) argues, Japanese robotics has sometime preferred minimal design rather than that of an android, the former:

which relies on underdetermined and implicit social cues that are given meaning through interaction. Nobuyoshi et al. call this the "subtractive method"—removing all but the most necessary communicative features to engage "the human drive to relate to others." (Šabanović 2010, 8)

If we were to redraw Mori's ontological horizon in his diagram reproduced above with a more Heideggerian emphasis, one direction of the axis of pathos might lead toward sympathy proper and the other end toward repulsion, with sympathy having various narcissistic forms, including sympathy toward animal companions and inanimate objects (especially those that resemble humans and pets).

Such would be a spectrum of human affect that describes one of the ways in which humans and other beings share a world. Android robots, as well as other robots that rely upon human mimesis or similitude for their functioning (such as Paro, the robotic seal used in nursing homes, among other sites, in order to provide possible comfort to those living there who are often very lonely and/or cognitively disabled), depend upon sympathetic human affective identifications and projections in order to increase their communicative use by human subjects. Our "Turing Test" of android robotics would test the communicational and emotional relations born from spectral appearances and their affective bonds. However, such a "test" must also take into account the willingness of humans to immediately work with or forgive the human "flaws" of such machines so as to consider them useful. Whether usefulness is seen as the criteria for what constitutes another human being, or another being more generally, depends upon the social and cultural psychologies involved and the moral and ethical assumptions of a culture. Many have argued that technological modernity, and both capitalism and the bureaucratic state, increase the tendency to see and treat others instrumentally. The step to a documentary understanding of otherness in some ways may, perhaps, increase this tendency, not only through the understanding of others as evidence for some theoretical or practical thesis and telos, but through the understanding of the self as such, as well (at least in its public presentations). The charms of individual uniqueness and quirkiness, charms that we all have not only because of our strengths, but from the singular combinations of our strengths and weaknesses, are difficult to replicate in not only designed systems, but also through systems that depend upon standards of norms for the production of expressions. While moral codes and bureaucratic and documentary systems may value consistency in appearance, experience and literature show us that our emotions often sympathize with those who are just like us, namely, less than consistent in the totality of our values and actions.

It may be that long-term, beneficial relationships with androids would lead to the overcoming of the uncanny valley (MacDorman and Cowley 2006). The case of Paro (the robotic seal that has been tested in nursing homes) shows how adults—in the absence of the affection of other people, ill, and alone in an emotionally devoid world of demeaning simulacrum and bureaucracy—can turn to inanimate objects as part-objects for expressing affection. (Indeed, fiction readers use stories and their characters as part-objects, as well.) It is no coincidence, then, as leisure time and wealth have risen and social fragmentation has increased in modernity, that domestic animals have been admitted into companion status in family households in "developed" countries (where, in the bourgeois world, affection is open to its most intense display), and subsequently a greater sympathy with these fellow beings has arisen among such people. As was said in the old adage "custom seduces us all," and here the custom is that of the adaptation of personal needs to whatever affordances of *Mitsein* there may be in our environments. Instrumental relations of all sorts take place in the prior opening of *Mitsein*, which is the human ontological precondition to all relations and all emotional feelings, positive or negative. There is no ontological predisposition toward a non-social human being; even being what we call "non-social" is a mode of being with other people, vis-à-vis their rejection or absence. Ontologically speaking, humans are always already "insympathy" with one another and with other beings, whether we are then, ontically speaking, sympathetic or unsympathetic, loving or hating one another or ourselves. Pathos—being concerned with one another and with ourselves—is our way of being with one another and being with ourselves, as beings who are fundamentally *Mitsein*. Pathos befalls us by the fact of our very mode of being existent.

While, like Sherry Turkle (2011), we might judge as morally degenerative the use of these objects as substitutes for human affection, technology is in some respects a tool for fulfilling all sorts of needs, which then may come to support, reinforce, and extend those needs. While we may find human attention and affection toward robots to be morally degenerative and infantile, no doubt similar views may be held by persons from other cultures who do not share our sense of domestic pets, for example, and they may wonder why we raise some animals to eat and others to have as companions and friends. The evolution of human psychological-technological transference continues, though we are wise to mark the differences with the various "others" involved for the important reason of not confusing both the extreme uniqueness and the fragility of life in the universe with the narcissism of our own instrumental needs. While higher order life forms, as all other beings and objects, have served humans, like all life we are but fragile moments in an otherwise inorganic vastness of the universe and even our own planet. Humans have the ability to make cognitive, practical, and aesthetic judgments and to be wrong with these (unlike machines, these judgments cannot solely be accounted for by attributing them to others' judgments and actions, nor can our wrongness simply be viewed as incorrectness to rules for actions). But, seemingly paradoxically, especially in the failure of the Turing Test of human similitude, this too is what androids can show us.

With androids, and particularly with geminoids (robotic replicas of living persons), our psychological projections are mediated and turned back upon subject positions of the self. In order to interact with machines, we must act like machines—often restricting our range of expression. Here, the self is understood not only as a person (that is, as an individual of normative rules and roles), but moreover this person acts as a rather "stiff" person, whose capacity for human action and judgment has been narrowed. This is a continuation of the documentary dialectic that we have earlier seen as an outcome of cultural self-inscriptions and social self-positionings in documentary systems.

The dialectics of human self-constitution and the attribution of living qualities to other beings (or their being devoid of such) arise from sympathetic relationships to other beings that involve their being seen like the self, as well as being seen like other persons. How strongly this self is seen as a hypothetical potential or as a person within social categories of rules and roles seems to depend not only on the different cultural and social psychologies that individuals inhabit, but also on the different personal beliefs and experiences that an individual has.

Whatever the culture and society, however, the appearance of another is important for personal formation and for communication. The nature of those others, directly or indirectly, will condition the type of individual that emerges and will affect his or her happiness or sadness in life. The other is not a slave to me, even if it is a robot, but rather, my identity is enslaved to him, her, or it, because I am, at core, a responsive and responsible being. This core is expressed through my psychological index, which gives me my abilities to act, think, and judge. This core is developed through experiences and especially through experiences with other human beings. I am not just similar to the other—I am the other—not in all their specificities, but in terms of their affects. And so, it is important that I understand the other who makes up who I am, or if that other is a robot, which I design or is designed to be with me, as other.

But further, it remains to be determined how androids will give or take away from the alterity or "Otherness" of who we are as human beings and as conscious being more generally, and which unite us as people and as conscious beings, and also gives us our singularity as the selves that we are. For the other just doesn't give me my person through giving me experiences, but also gives me my self, the mystery of my life, through both their lives and their deaths, which both proceed and come after me, as a radical Otherness that haunts and composes each of ourselves and who each of us is. This "test" would be too much for even what I have called an "android Turing Test," and so would leave androids to being something like a toy or stuffed animal, rather than even a real one or a human being. For this "Otherness" cannot be tested for, but rather it is a condition, literally given to us by our being. Androids would remain then, what they are, always an analogy, though like all analogies they could be incorporated into and extend chains of symbolic substitutions.

The Dialects of Intersubjective Affect

The constitution of the self via others has been well known and recognized throughout time. Konrad Lorenz gave the formal name of "imprinting" to the ability of another to shape the formation of the self in psychological development. The dialectic of self and other was shown by Lorenz to be based on a natural social bonding affect. As Hegel (1977) argued, self-consciousness is constituted by its "becoming" through others.

Jacques Lacan argued that imprinting is performed in two stages. First, through the mirror stage, dominated by the imaginary order, when the young child is imprinted as a unified individual through his or her image in a mirror (an "objective" image that therefore assumes an ego-ideal). And second, later in life within the symbolic order, through which the other and the self is constituted not by a narcissistic relationship to the image or imagination, but by an Otherness of language, which precedes the individual and gives him or her a subjectivity that goes beyond the narcissism of the mirror image.

The importance of the mirror stage (Lacan 2006) lies in it being a dialectically constituted identification of the self by an image that is both *of the self* and *not myself*. The mirror stage involves not simply a repetition of myself, but also the introjection of the other into self-consciousness in the return of consciousness to its self via the other (though in the mirror stage, narcissistically).

At the heart of Lacan's analysis of the mirror stage, as well as throughout Lacan's entire work, there is Hegel's dialectic of consciousness (Hegel 1977): My consciousness of the other, for example, as the other of myself which I try to understand, and in trying to understand gives me also a view upon myself that sees me as an object of another's perspective, splits my identity into two (self and personhood). Through the other, the self returns to its consciousness as self-conscious. This is what Lacan called the "split" nature of subjectivity. (Which, it might be added, also allows Lacan to reintroduce alterity despite the dialectic of consciousness seeming to close it off, as both the other person and myself are constituted and marked by language and other alterities that precede and come after them. In other words, the particular concept of being that forms particular types of consciousness and self-consciousness, is *marked* in its very composition, as a question, as the mystery of, what type of being one is and can be).

As a developmental psychology, psychoanalysis views the earlier stages of life as never being fully abandoned. The mirror stage is never fully left, but instead, can form various projective relationships with the world. In Lacan's late work, the Borromean knot symbolizes the intertwining—and mutually supporting—role of the three orders (the real, imaginary, and symbolic) in supporting the subject. The complete undoing of these knots from one another can be found in psychotic patients.

As Lacan writes in his 1949 "The Mirror Stage as Formative of the *I* Function," the split identity of the subject is itself filled with "phantoms" that make up its identity (Lacan 2006). In this way the ego (*das Ich*—the I) from the mirror stage onward is haunted, not least by the spectral phantom of a unified person that appears to me and which I fantasize as my own image. Arguably, this is what a geminoid of myself could represent and which, by analogy, would form part of the uncanniness of androids in general. It would be an idealized me—idealized by a technological dream—but lacking in almost all respects. (And so, perhaps even more forgivable, than if it was a copy of someone else.)

Lacan discusses the process of identification in the mirror stage in the quote below. The quote's syntactical style (both in the original, and, sensitive to this, in the English translation) rhetorically performs the dialectical movements of identification that he is discussing:

For the total form of his body, by which the subject anticipates the maturation of his power in a mirage, is given to him only as a gestalt, that is, in an exteriority in which, to be sure, this form is more constitutive than constituted, but in which, above all, it appears to him as the contour of his stature that freezes it and in a symmetry that reverses it, in opposition to the turbulent movements with which the subject feels he animates it. Through these two aspects of its appearance, this gestalt—whose power should be considered linked to the species, though its motor style is as yet unrecognizable—symbolizes the *I*'s mental permanence, at the same time as it prefigures its alienating destination. This gestalt is also replete with the correspondences that unite the *I* with the statue onto which man projects himself, the phantoms that dominate him, and the automaton with which the world of his own making tends to achieve fruition in an ambiguous relation. (Lacan 2006, 76–77)

Through the image of another who is both who I am and not who I am, the mirror state prefigures the split subject that more fully occurs in the symbolic order, in which the I is split not by an image, but by the affordances of language; not by the other, but by the Other within and by which both myself and others understand and express one another and ourselves. It constitutes an ego-ideal of a different nature than in the mirror stage, one that precedes my being but constitutes it, given by the parents first of all, who form the subject's first and most lasting voice of not only conscience, but also consciousness. Whereas the ego-ideal of the mirror stage appears as attainable, that of the symbolic remains a mystery to the subject, lying not in subjectivity per se, not in conceptual or documentary denotation, but in linguistic and other expressive performances; not the referents of the symbolic, but the fact of the symbolic itself as an event, including the traces of the self as it temporally folds and unfolds.

From a psychoanalytic perspective, in order to approach being a similar life form to humans, androids would at least have to gain both the imagination of a unified self and the alienation of a split subject in order to replicate the developmental experience of a young child. But, the construction of the I in such a form is a delicate affair in any subject's experience, much less a project for human design.

Phoebe Sengers (2002), for example, has argued that AI agents suffer from a fragmented, "schizophrenic," lack of narrative coherence. For Kant in his *Critique of Pure Reason* it is the unity of apperception as an a priori condition for any understanding that forms the coherence of the subject. The continuity and unity of space, time, and causality in apperception are the affordances for the continuous and complementary unification of perspectives and voices that constitute the expressive powers (or "language") of a normally maturing and mature self. However, for Lacan, in a more Hegelian mode than Kant, of course, these a priori conditions only appear from out of relationships with other subjects, who demand of the subject a continuous voice and a point of view. In other words, the formal conditions of apperception are a product of the subject's historical experience with other human beings and their demands for temporal, spatial, and logical continuity.

As is well known in studies of isolation, the self becomes disassembled without another to which it is made *repons*ible. The other, here, appears as a north star through which my own identity and expressions are structured with place, time, and direction, and whose expression then returns to me as a presence that gives to not only others, but to me as well, a sense of personal history and a certain feeling or hope of rationality, common sense, and righteousness, whatever the real qualities of my expressions may ultimately turn out to be. We diangulate or triangulate (if we include or exclude from our accounts the cultural forms and social norms—i.e., the logic—by which the dialectic occurs) our meaning and sense by means of both the other's expressions and categories and the other's responses to our utterances and actions. Without such cultural and social positioning existence takes the phenomenological form of dreams, or in waking life the doubts of the neurotic or even worse, of multiple personalities or of schizophrenic schisms—various voices and perspectives that train wreck in a single utterance.

As in Freud's works, Lacan's works recognize an early developmental narcissism as intrinsic, rather than pathological, and as necessary for the formation of the I as a split, but also continuous subject. This narcissism of desire through the imagination, as a projective catharsis, is necessary for both the subject and the other to appear, and it is the prefiguration in the subject of an alterity or Otherness that will inhabit and position the self and others as consciousnesses capable of understanding and misunderstanding. And yet, with robots as with all readings of data expressions, this very psychological basis for knowledge leads to what Ekbia (2008) calls in the context of AI an "attribution fallacy"—namely, the attribution of human personhood, and even human selfhood, to machines.

What prevents imaginative projection from being turned into an adult form of unadulterated narcissism is the other's resistance to it, at least at the level of the autonomy of agency. This autonomy is in the form of powers that are not necessarily forced back upon the subject him- or herself, but rather, a product of the other's own expressive powers—"power" in the form of generation or expression. The generative, and not necessarily the repressive, powers of the other are what gives the other his or her resistance to the narcissism that is the subject's "needing to know" from the other its own needs. And it is this resistance, in agreeable, hostile, careful, or confused terms, that makes the other's information to be knowledge for the subject.

More specifically, it is the expressiveness of the other according to the other's own wishes and whims, the possession of his or her *own time* (and not only needs) that checks the subject's narcissism and is the cause for the narcissist's own frustrations and anxieties, whose desire races around to find various easier sources for attention. This essential lack of full autonomy, this lack of being aware of themselves as temporal beings for whom one's time is essentially each their own, is what robots most phenomenologically lack and is in no small part why we lose respect for them as human equals and why we find those who act like them to be somewhat odd or pathetic. When we are forced to be with them, such robots (or people acting like such) are present as instrumental means to ends, not as ends themselves. They appear to us as alien or (self-) alienated affects, or simply as tools. And for this reason, as well, friends treating us in this way are eventually disdained.

The Ontological Constitution of Subjects and Objects

Both primary (intrinsic to the agent) and secondary (contextual) powers or affordances work in reciprocal relation to one another in the constitution of beings and things as potential and actualized powers of expression. Psychoanalysis is rich in expressing this through expressions that follow an "inner" and "outer" topology: in notions such as repression and introjection, "outer" contents to the mind (secondary affordances) are conceptualized as being internalized as "unconscious" powers of the self (primary affordances).

We could see situations of expression as composed of three types of powers of affordances: cultural, social, and physical. Things or objects proper have only physical powers of affordance, and only in very determinate situations for their expression. (I avoid the term "material" here since cultural, social, and physical powers each have their "material" dimension—that is, they have affective force and resistance in relation to other powers and bodies.) Primary affordances or powers are part of the agent, either biologically constituted or formed through experience and learning. Secondary affordances or powers exist in the situational context of an expression and allow and shape it. Acts can often be accounted for by attributing them to primary or secondary causal powers, or most often to both to various degrees. Learning creates primary powers as well as biologically inherent properties of a body. In addition, intersubjective affective relations in situations constitute a "horizontal" input of forces that, too, may act upon an agent; they traverse the subject, as the subject of expressive powers in a situation (Day 2011).

The expressive powers of a being—made up its experiences and its personal skills (its expressive "toolbox" built from experience)—constitute each individual as a unique singularity of expressive traits—a self. Just as individuals develop into singular selves over time, with their own traits, preferences, and powers, so do species, though with sometimes poorly defined, but still real, sets of unique demonstrable powers. In short, the ontological constitution of beings as sets of powers is evolutionary and developmental, shaped and afforded by the powers of their environment and the pressures put upon and shaping the beings concerned. A funda-mental ontology describes general ways of being for types of being; the exact expressions that make this up are singular, though cultural forms, social norms, and of course physical characteristics most of all (at least in larger species) are remarkably resilient and slow to change.

Intentionality and Situations

The central ontological problem for robots as AI agents and how they relate to human beings is how they are constituted as powers of expression. Such a problem leads to the problem of intention, since intention is, generally, the problem of the self-aware deployment of powers in a situation. It is thus reasonable to ask what is the source of intentions, and whether robots can exhibit intentions. Can robots intend to do things? Is "wanting" something possible for robots? And, moreover, could we ask if a broader and even "unconscious" form of wanting (in the broader, Lacanian psychoanalytical sense of desire) is possible for a robot? Fulfilling these conditions would be part of the affective Turing Test for an android.

In traditional AI, agency was constituted through formal design, but the problem has been that of anticipating all possible situations for response and expression and then making an agent that is flexible enough to gener-ate new expressions in novel situations. Simply put, in place of experience and evolution there has been the attempt to design agency as an a priori, formal, document made up of logical statements. More recent works have attempted to produce agents that learn (Ekbia 2008), but even when these systems have been technically successful the question remains of whether such machine activities constitute learning in the sense that we use this term with human activities.

Japanese android creations, such as Professor Ishiguro's Geminoid and Geminoid-F, have been premised on mechanical design and a rather primi-tive form of what we can call "communicative AI," based on formally designed mechanical movements, physical and verbal scripts, and some-times human agents speaking telephonically through microphones in the androids. More developed forms presumably would occur not exclusively through programming, but through machine learning, where AI commu-nicative patterns are recursively developed through the mass sampling of real human expressions. Androids may play a particularly important role in their appearance as human beings, allowing human beings to interact with them as naturally as they would with other human beings, thus increasing the robots' learning abilities.

Communicative AI can be seen from two aspects: robots "seducing" human beings into feeling that human or humanlike communication is occurring (which may then produce Ekbia's (2008) "attribution fallacy") and robots learning through communication. This learning can both be through physical movements (if the physical design affords such) and through speech and other expressive acts.

If learning does occur and agency is shown as a result of this, then we must ask if the robots or androids will be judged as acting as selves or persons. For Karl F. MacDorman and Stephen J. Cowley (2006), personhood for robots is established by their exhibiting three qualities: the agent's ability to construct its own identity, assume different roles, and discriminate in forming friendship. As I have been using the term within a more narrow and normative context, distinguishing it from the concept of the self, "personhood" involves the agent fitting into normative rules and roles for expression. The first and third of MacDorman and Cowley's named qualities are rather properties of what I have been calling, after Harré (1989), the "self": the hypothetical potentiality of a unique and singular agent of powers.

We often assert that such a self exists if the individual seems to show to us intentionality—that is, if we posit a causality to actions beyond strictly normative rules and roles so that the agent is assigned unique manners of combining cultural forms and social norms in what we deem to be *individuality, choice, personality, style,* and *character.* The self constitutes an apperceptive singularity beyond formal rules and roles, per se, and instead, is seen as the point from which rules and roles are deployed. This deployment and the reasons that the subject gives for such constitutes intentionality and the explanation of intentions, and these are seen as signs of there being a self. With robots, this may have to come about more by something like machine learning than through formal programming. We still have much to learn, however, about how rules and roles are combined and chosen by singular selves as they develop, and how they are deployed, especially in ambiguous situations.

Commonly, intentions are seen as being the "causes" of a subject's expressions. Finding such "causes," however, can be not only difficult, but also problematic, as can be seen in moral psychology or legal cases, for example, which seek to find the cause or reasons for an act. Normatively, such causes are sought in norms or "rules" for particular acts. But the problem is: What secondary set of rules or judgments arbitrate the choices of primary judgments, which result in publicly recognized acts? For example, I have a choice of doing x, y, or z, and I choose to act in such a way that z is done. What rule led me to make this choice? And, of course, was there a rule in this choice or was the decision made out of sympathy or from simply copying another's actions (correctly or erroneously) or from a misinterpretation? Could these be called "rules"? At a certain point, as well, even rule-based behavior becomes habitual. Do we then say that we "choose" option z rather than x or y?

The problem with normative ethics in the sense of the above is that norms are seen as part of a self. This is not a problem per se, since it simply says the common sense notion that the self is a toolbox of available devices used for doing tasks (including among those tools, rules of use). The problem occurs if we then say that this self then has another self (or set of tools) to arbitrate what "tools" are used in a given situation. What then, we could ask, arbitrates that choice? And so the regression of sets of rules for other sets of rules could go on and on—*reductio ad absurdum*—if we see the self as a purely formal construct.

We could reply to this last criticism by saying that there is only one toolbox—the self as a focal point for singularly collected skills and tools—but that the tools or skills exist not as sets of formal hierarchies, but rather, as a sort of bricolage of potential, situationally deployed assets. The model of mind then shifts from that of being a formal, hierarchical, model of analytic code to a situational choosing of tools that may have multiple dimensions of relation, including, but not limited to, analytical hierarchies, in response to situational needs, which too may give tools for the subject's expressions. This corresponds to something closer to the model of users in newer, more situational and mobile, information systems. Duplicating this in an android form, and in a communicational situation, however, is challenging, of course.

One of the founding principles of psychoanalysis is that people are not always "conscious" of the reasons for (or rules by) which they do things. The explanation for this according to psychoanalytical theory is that some reasons lie in an unconscious "region" (according to Freud's topographic model, at least) of the mind.

We can, however, interpret intentions through a more Lacanian notion of the unconscious, one that uses dialectic to view the subject and its intentions (desires and needs) as a function of communication in situations, rather than view intention as unidirectional "causes" for the subject's expressions. Such an explanation would also expand the notion of "intention" from goal-oriented actions to more general classes of agent-powered actions. Communication occurs in webs of relations, including the self's own self-conversations, as both vocally and subvocally (i.e., "thought") performed.

Ancient Greek rhetoricians had a term for the need of persons to tailor their remarks to a situation and an audience: *kairós. Kairós* was the moment that the truth was revealed to the audience—that the audience became convinced as to the true meaning of what the speaker was saying. In other words, the audience *and* the speaker appear in the moment of *kairós* as common identities in a "field" of meaning and potential communication. At that moment, both believe that they can understand each other—that something real was being pointed to by the speaker's words. At the moment of *kairós* the speaker gathers him or herself, together with the audience, into a way of understanding a situation. Both the speech act and what is being spoken of become evident in an *event* of truth.

Ancient rhetoricians understood something that has evaded more formalistic understandings of the mind. Namely, that minds don't "begin" from subjects, but rather, that subjects and their minds are situated as expressions within webs of relational affordances that span across private and public notions of individuals and across past, present, and potentially future events. Even highly formal hierarchies of actions are situational. The military demands that its soldiers act according to "orders" or explicit rules and engineers are expected to build bridges according to bridge-engineering principles. But, even these rather strict and formal acts require that a person or persons understanding a situation so that the acts can be correctly performed *within and in accordance with situations.*

Thus, the rules and norms that structure a subject's acts come from both situational affordances and "internal" norms; both may be measures of "correct" acts, and so the "correct" act may well be a compromise that neither exactly corresponds to prior judgments and experience nor, perhaps, to certain "objective" measures of a situation. Both the subject's expressive appearances and the object's meanings are pulled into appearance by the logic and language of the situation. In a *kairós*, the situation *is* for the subject(s), because both the subject(s) and the "contents" of the situation have been historically assembled together, for all the subjects' understandings. The preacher and the believers reach the moment of *kairós* because they believe together in what they see and have seen, speak, and have heard, and these together—the seers and the seen—*are* the situation, and they hold within such the subject(s) and their objects *together*.

But, is the *kairós* of the situation logical, and if not logical, at least reasonable? Is this reasonableness achieved through correspondence with rules and roles? In regard to robots, because one is still dealing largely with programmed machines, the matter comes down to an issue of *scripts* that *inscribe* both the subject and others within them. But, as mentioned previously, it is not only conformity to a script but also nonconformity to (or individualization of) scripts, which we demand that other things show in order to treat them as beings. This difference, which distinguishes subjects from objects, this problem of rhythm and moods for expression, are put to the test with androids on multiple (physical, verbal, cognitive) horizons, which together form the problem of the *affect* of a near-living document— its total affective information as it were. The move from formalized scripts or documents to communicational documentarity, where speech acts in communicational exchanges are used as documents for further speech acts in communicational exchanges, is the mechanism of what I have been calling "communicational AI," and where, I would suggest, that android appearances may make the most sense, at least in physically live contexts.

Performing Androids and Ethical Choice

One would think that theater would be an ideal place to understand how humans and androids could interact in a scripted environment. In theater, both are scripted. Indeed, in a twenty-minute play, Professor Hiroshi Ishiguro's Geminoid-F has played the role, sort of speaking, of a female android— which it is, however (Guizzo, 2010). The popular press reported "her" performance as "stiff," with its human actress counterpart reportedly saying, "There's a bit of distance. The robot has a quite particular position because it's got a voice, but it's not some kind of human presence" (Oh 2010).

While scripted activities with robots may increase their abilities to be interactive partners in task-based activities, and having an android "play" an android is not any great dramatic feat (since that is what it is anyway), theatrical performances like this help show just how far even scripted performances have to go in creating a symbiosis between android and humans that might satisfy an android Turing Test.

Realist theatrical "performances" literally play between scripted narratives and presented gestures, pulling the audience into narrated representations and "live" appeals simultaneously. The emotional appeal lies in both a suspension of disbelief in the narrative and a belief in a performance of live gestures. The actors and actresses *make real* a script by situating themselves between the script and the audience's beliefs and feelings. This is the appeal that gives the play its realism.

In theater, performances occur before the audience, in the mode of representation. "Need" is performed, rather than had, for not only the audience but for the actors and actresses. But it is here that androids most fail to appear as human.

Why? In terms of information androids fail to provide the fulfillment of a need. What is that need in theater? That need is to answer to a call of being an intentional agent, even within a script. The "acting" of the actors and actresses consists in emphasizing by facial and other gestures the *undecidability* of the acts in the play, even when we know in advance (as in classical theater, from Aeschylus to Shakespeare) the probable destiny of the main characters' actions. It is precisely in this difference between script and performance, between destiny and the human act that the audience feels identifications with the actors and actresses and that the actors and actresses can "connect" with one another. In other words, theater shows us that it is our choices, despite our probable and necessary unfolding destinies (the most certain being death), that make us beings, and most acutely, human beings. This is what makes up tragedy and comedy. No machine, at least today, could ever have these same destinies. And so compared to a great actor or actress in a great role—who can bring out this difference between what can and may or shall be and what is actually performed, in both the difference between the script and the gestures and words, and between the foreshadowing and the character's present actions—the machine will fail to be anything other than a documentary supplement, performing its own supplementarity as a document within the very *play* of difference that is the tragedy or comedy. What the play tells us is that however scripted we think that we are or may be, what is at play is precisely the play itself, or life.

Many judgments of AI agents are founded upon a narrow view of what constitutes human performance or *acting*, in general. But the reading of scripts in acting is not often seen as genuine acting, because acting is seen as something more than the reading of scripts, as something more than simply *Darstellung*. In the *kairós* of the gesture there is a positioning of one's own agency with others. *This is the performance*—onstage and offstage. It is the making present of meaning within a relation of the self and others. What is being referred to is not only what is referenced by the actor or actress, but the difference between what they refer to and what the drama's entire unfolding refers to. This is the *play* of signification in drama that gives the drama meaning.

In the same way, ethical acts lie not in the following of moral rules (i.e., the following of scripts or prescriptions—"do not lie," etc.), but rather, in the choosing of moral rules and roles in regard to situations. We do not judge just the rightness or wrongness of ethical actions, but rather, the genuineness of ethical (rather than moral) intent, based on values of good faith and judgment and based on our experiences in similar situations (situations that are not clearly decidable as to the wisdom and outcome of a choice of an action). What is ethically most interesting is not the person who chooses between good and bad, but between bad and worse, or where good or bad outcomes are unclear for a choice of action. Drama shows us that even the best of choices can result in terrible outcomes, and that sometimes there are only terrible outcomes among which we must choose the best option. And comedy shows us that even if we choose badly it may result in favorable outcomes or at least entertaining ones. But in all these cases, the most acute values of choice, and therefore of human (and probably other higher animal) action, lies in the space between necessity and action, particularly within indeterminate situations. This indeterminateness gives to human being the quality of radical temporality, choice and what is sometimes referred to in the Western cultural tradition as "free will." With a single action, the future—and our retrospective understanding of the past and who we are in the present—may change. For human beings their own senses of time originate from their actions in or out of such crucial *kairós* or situations. Time may "drag on" or "pass rapidly" within a situation and a situation may restructure the everyday pace of time "passing." Psychological time is not physical time, and so the gulf between the "life" of the experientially formed agent and the programmed one that doesn't experience time as its own is huge.

It is the ethical choices in drama that rivet us. It is not a measure of simple correctness, but of human fallibility and human choosing (and the choices that other higher order animals make, too, which also give them individual characteristics); of finite and unclear agency and of free will, and of life or "time" as it emerges out of these singular experiences. One has a genuine life, one is a person of qualities, only where, at least on occasion, the making of choices is both clear and unclear; one must act, but there is no guarantee of a favorable outcome. But on the other hand, this lack of guarantee is only there because of the necessity of having to act, and thus, having to choose.

Documents as Fulfilling a Need

We often speak of documents as fulfilling a need, but as we have seen in the preceding chapters, needs are structured by documents within social and political economies of need. Perhaps more as supplements, than as attempts to overcome the "uncanny valley" in all aspects of human duplication, android robots can assume a possible place on the ontological horizon of human experience. However, the very likeness of androids to humans sometimes disrupts such supplementarity.

As can be seen in the case of Paro, the robotic seal, in the setting of nursing homes, certain human agents, either because of cognitive deficiencies or because of emotional needs and situational limits upon satisfying those needs, are drawn toward such objects, and taken as beings, for the fulfillment of their needs. In such an environment Paro takes its place with much of the rest of the domestic animal kingdom, which has unknowingly constituted themselves, in part, as what psychoanalysis calls "part-objects" to human beings. Part-objects capture subjects in terms of needs and they act as metonymical substitutes for the needed object as a whole. What is important here is that while a deficient whole may elicit fear (i.e., the uncanny valley), the part, when scripted into a need, may be taken up without hesitation as a tool. This is true whether we are referring to stuffed animals, artificial limbs, or anything else taken to various extents as tools that help fulfill needs. Scripts may be symbolic or physical actions that define the object's information for a need in a way that mediates between the vast discrepancy between machine and personal agency. Like the "training" of domestic pets, both the "owner" and the "pet" need to be trained together. They are scripted together so as to reduce the uncanny valley. They express themselves together through common affordances and interactions, like documents and users.

But this also tells us something very important about the documentary positioning of human beings, as well. Humans and other higher forms of life are valued for the indeterminacy and the choices that they make. There may be ethical choices expressed through the partial or total functions of information systems (e.g., human-controlled drone attacks), but these do not take place in the systems themselves, but somewhere along the chain of production involving their design and use by human beings. Choices between scripts are perhaps not reducible to scripts. As has been argued, there seems to be an essence of indetermination to each individual, a singularity of experience, relations to the world, and expressions that may require documentary information but are not themselves reducible to documentary information. And conversely, data and documents may not always tell us a lot about the values of a person. Despite the predilection to reduce all knowledge and art to "information" (Heidegger 1977b), and today to data representation, such a reduction does very little to address what literature and art express as knowledge. As I have suggested, it is because literature and art, as well as human beings, express the tensions between what is and what may or shall be.

Critiques, such as Sherry Turkle's (2011), fit within a long tradition of warning us about the dangers of being seduced by artificial agents; a seduction at the cost of ignoring or reducing the value of those beings that have a living agency, who "push back" against the narcissism of needs by the powers of their chosen expressions. "Robotic animals" and "robotic humans"— in the sense of both robots and androids proper, and restrictively trained and self-trained animals and humans—tend to work well with human agents in instrumental or task-based systems because of two aspects: first, the robots can be designed to fulfill set needs, and second, humans compensate for the limited expressions of robots by adapting to them. Only more recently have machines come to approach the flexibility of human agents in more complex and adaptive tasks. Turkle's concern seems to be that human adaptation to machine design fulfills needs in a narcissistic manner, since the machines are designed to fulfill needs without "push back" and humans adapt to machine systems in ways that then limit their experiences with other people. While it is the case that human beings who treat other animals well often tend to treat human beings well, history and experience show us that the contrary may be the case as well—that those tender affections extended to the easily submissive or "domestic" human and/or nonhuman animals or to those that win our affections by their very loyalty or mere appearance may lead to hatred or sadism when encountering the real world of other human beings with different or contrary customs or opinions than our own. Turkle's (2011) fear is that humans will be captured in technological systems that are imaginative reductions; images, objects, and altogether screens for consciousness that have been designed to fulfill personal needs without challenging those needs in terms of not only the needs, but also more importantly, the singular being, of others. Thus, human existence as mediated by technical systems will result in the narrowing of human beings as singular individual and group *potentialities* by algorithms of known *possibilities*. This is a documentary fear that extends back to Plato's complaints about writing in his *Phaedrus*, but has been given a stronger technological and a broader sociological power by modern documentary systems.

That one could be seduced by the very part-objects that one takes as meaningful, however, should not be surprising. In regard to other animals, the ability of these other animals to appear or act like human infants, as well as fit within human communicative patterns, is often taken by people as the key characteristic for their being treated more *humanely*, rather than their being taken as some form of "dumb" (both intellectually stupid and unable to speak) animals and in various ways being seen as "ready-to-hand" (Heidegger 1962) and what we could call, "ready-to-eat." (The transition from being placed in the latter to being placed in the former categories has saved some members of animal species and even the species itself from extinction—in our own time, witness the fate of the dolphin in Western countries, now further protected by "dolphin-safe fishing" campaigns.) As well, the lack of such feelings has formerly relegated other human beings to being "dumb animals" (i.e., slaves, enemies, lower subordinates) in relation to those who rule. Whatever the basis for the communicative illusion of complete understanding (whether it takes place between humans and other animals or, for Lacan, between the human sexes in what he ironically refers to as *méconnaissance*), nonetheless we see everyday that pragmatic and satisfactory communication leading to good-enough understanding and respect for the otherness of the other can result in the greater sharing of physical space and to the emotive bonds of human care.

But because we are such communicational animals within our own "species-being" (Marx) and because we have mastered the representation of the entire earth so well, we tend to view communication in terms of that which is like us or not, until proven otherwise. The AI and android "attribution fallacies" (Ekbia 2008) are cases where we may see the seductive qualities that our own fantasies have upon us when projected onto another that is not another being, but an object.

All these examples read upon the "other" a communicative *evidence* which allows them to be seen as a *human* or *rational* part of the universe: in our thought of them as part of our communicative circuit they become evidence of something more than they were before and so they may be spared some of their previous historical or other cultural fates as slaves to our whims and/or, in the case of other animals (though sometimes human beings as well in some cultures), meals on our table.

If, like in the use of Paro, the goal is increased communication and displayed affectivity in a context where its lack is harmful to persons, then androids may lose ethical objections attributed to their use. Pathological attachments to them become just one more pathological attachment, not so different than with any other part-object. We *read* into their thinghood the being that we wish to see as their expressed content; in other words, we read them in terms of their use to us, their user.

All this is to say that these part-objects inhabit ontological places within the human political economies of value and use in which they are placed. What type of "being" that they will be for people depends on how their thinghood is read, which does depend upon design of course, but largely depends upon their belonging within economies of need so that they may be seen as *useful things*. The transgression that really concerns Turkle (2011) seems to be that of passing from a respect economy (other beings "push back" and "demand respect" in terms of their autonomy) to an instrumental economy (where beings are understood as "mere tools" or things) via our increasing technological mediation with the world, and the forgetting of this transgression in a social regime of instrumental relationships. As we have been charting throughout the modern documentary tradition, this is the taking of beings for things and things for being in the service of information needs by a user.

If we did want to design machines to really pass an android Turing Test, then we would have to try and design machines that don't mimic normative (that is to say, "rational") actions, but rather, what is specific to humans, so-called irrational actions: choices being made and justified when it isn't clear what the outcome of an action is or what constitutes a best choice; irrational behavior where rational judgment is thrown out the window; neuroses. Not actions devoid of logic, but devoid of a normative sense of rationality or reason; actions born, as it were, of intuition and even faith.

The singularity of beings still poses an enigma to be conquered by information system design. This will be the topic of my final two chapters: how "big data" attempts to comprehend the singularity of human beings and what this means for governance, intellectual freedom, and the West's Enlightenment tradition of critique.

6 Governing Expression: Social Big Data and Neoliberalism

In the last chapter, I presented a picture of individual human beings (and also other beings to various extents) as made up of unique and singular personal "toolboxes" of potential "powers" or skills of expressions. These powers are derived through the unique experiences that each individual has and their ways of understanding. To begin this chapter, I would like to contrast this view with the concept of persons as labor commodities in markets regulated by exchange value (Marx 1977), where these very issues of quality are translated into quantitative measures in order to assure the ability of labor and products to be measured in complex markets of commodity exchange. (Where the equality of items x and y are further mediated by the abstract entity of z, namely money, as the foundational concept of capital.) For such exchanges, money represents not only the means for exchange, but it represents, not least through the societal-wide extension of concepts like "the market," the expansion of commodity exchange value to life as a whole. In the first part of this chapter I would like to investigate neoliberalism's informational reformation of the "spirit" of personal and social psychology, or what in psychoanalysis is called "the drive."

As is well known, for Marx this system of quantification ultimately represented the abstraction of all human creative and expressive activities in that system (known as capitalism) of abstract exchange and commodification mediated by money, and it represented as well the subsumption of human beings (and other beings) in their individuality and sociality as having the "bottom line" value of being either direct or indirect producers and consumers in the capitalist market. For Marx, for this reason value in capitalism was not determined solely by the exchange of labor for the wage, but rather, was a product of "social labor" (Marx 1865/1969)—in other words, it was the product of the work of the social whole in the support and valorization of capitalism through paid and unpaid labor, as well as consumption. For capitalism, the entire life sphere is reducible to the logic of commodities in exchange, starting with the initial dialectical exchange of life quality into monetary quantity as mediated by the concept of money as a chief concept of value. Dialectically then, as well, quantity in capitalism (money) becomes a qualitative measure by the same yardstick (in fundamental notions of value in a capitalist society, such as being wealthy, being poor, being successful, being unsuccessful—all measured by amounts of money or monetary goods accumulated or had by an individual or group). While, of course, quantity of money is not the only source of pride and power in even a capitalist society, in a capitalist society with money comes power, and so too the pride that finds power as its *raison d'être.*

"The market" (and its logic, or "invisible hand") as both an abstract cultural notion and as concrete manners of exchange, thus remains largely untheorized in the discourse of everyday life, since it functions as the ideological norm and the infrastructure of our lives in capitalism. In modern capitalism, we have increasingly seen the mediation of life values into capitalist values take more and more abstract forms, not only in the processes of market exchanges, but even prior to such in human understanding and self-understanding.

For example, as was discussed earlier, today it is common to abstract one's self in order to put one's self "out there" on the Internet. One creates an "online identity" toward creating a "brand" for one's self, which may be exchanged for some other commodities (including other persons as such, as the logic of markets permeates through all human relationships—love, marriage, labor, etc., through contractual and customary legal arrangements). While the market in liberalism regulated goods and labor, in neoliberalism it regulates identity and an identity's expressions in almost every area of one's life sphere, because each area is seen as contributing to forming the competitive individual in the overall labor "marketplace."

The "entrepreneurial spirit" is celebrated in neoliberalism as the *Geist* of the entire life sphere, and it is increasingly becoming a necessity with the end of work (or more specifically, the end of employment) that is being seen in developed economies across the world. Within a scarcity environment (produced by wealth consolidation and technological advances) and the dismantling of the welfare state and the absence of a livable social wage, other values can't exist without this "bottom line" of market identification, which subsumes human life (and other animal and plant lives, and even the eco-system of the planet itself) at every stage and in every corner. However initially disruptive, digital technologies, like other new technologies, become increasingly adapted and exponentially empowering of the economy that pulls upon them as the "strange attractors" in their development and innovation. In the neoliberal economy, the subject must locate him- or herself, both technically and socially, within norms for predictability, which then feed back and reshape the subject's future expressions in public spaces.

And yet, as we have noted, the dialectic between the subject and documents within social information systems is, historically speaking, *progressive*: innovation is necessary in expressions for reasons of both the reproduction of the overall system of production and for the reassessment of lesser values (leading up to, if possible, their maximal capitalization, redesign, and redeployment in new circumstances, etc.). Dialectical relationships are not just logical and systemic, but also historical; evolution occurs. As Michel Foucault (2008) stressed in his work on neoliberalism, contemporary neoliberalism, unlike earlier market liberalism, is not just a celebration of the functions of markets, but rather, neoliberalism stresses *competition* as the means for the social value of markets. Neoliberal ideology asserts that markets innovate by means of competition, but it also asserts that markets foster social progress by doing such. Social progress for neoliberalism involves "freeing" individuals from "welfare states," that is, from prior forms of collective action and risk management, so that they can compete against one another. Like capitalism as a whole, neoliberalism is cheered as both a revolutionary and an evolutionary force that breaks up static economic and cultural blocks. Competition is seen as resulting in the most innovative and the least costly goods and in maximizing individual expression.

Thus, contemporary neoliberalism has offered a certain type of resolution to the problem of having *both* the Enlightenment demand for human freedom *and* the notion of capitalism and its reality of money as the organizing concept and the mediating logic for society and culture. Neoliberal policy and ideology has done this by rolling back the institutions of the modern bourgeois public sphere other than those institutions that are involved with commercial enterprise and the promotion of such. The resolution of both concrete freedom and abstract labor (and being) in capitalism involves the commoditization of the total life-sphere in terms of capitalism and its values (e.g., money, the marketplace, competition) and its logic (e.g., exchange value, commodification of persons and things). Public space is "freed" and in its place "the market" is said to regain its natural status as the *fundamental* condition of human being. And so in neoliberalism, the fundamental ontology of the individual is seen as that of the freely competing subject in the marketplace, with this last term spread out across and permeating all areas of life. Within contemporary neoliberalism, all institutions and forces of the neoliberal state—family, educational, cultural, social, and foremost political—must be oriented in this direction for the maximum good and fundamental freeing and salvation of individuals and society as a whole. From another point of view, though, this demand and its utopia may be read as resulting in a totalitarian economic state, in that all institutions and forces are read according to this "bottom line" value.

As authors in the Italian autonomist movements have argued for the past fifty and more years, this "total subsumption" of capital upon the life-sphere has been accomplished through "material" and "immaterial" means.[1] According to these authors, capital in late capitalism and neoliberalism has attempted to progressively colonize the entire life-sphere. Resistance, they argue, comes through the "reserves" to capital that remain as the social and intellectual foundation from which capital draws, including through "immaterial labor" using digital means. Gradually during modernity, such theorists have argued, life itself has been taken as a target for capitalist subsumption, through the cooptation of communication, sexual and familial relationships (Fortunati 1995), education, and every other sphere of human activity, with economic exchange and survival as the ultimate justification for all relationships. (Yet, interestingly, certain work practices remain as unpaid or poorly paid labor, not the least of those being labor in the home and in education. See Fortunati 1995.)

Capital's "apparatus of capture" has become increasingly efficient and broad in its appropriation of selves as subjects of its political economy through the combination of appropriating governmental functions such as: buying off political actors and agencies, cutting public funding to modernist institutions and infrastructures, redefining the agenda of education and other cultural institutions toward capitalist values, owning and narrowing the focus of the media, forcing family structures and individuals to adapt to scarcity economies, and using government police and surveillance forces and economic pressures to crush resistance. In short, it is said that neoliberalism has advanced by the totalitarian institutionalization of national and international capitalism, one nation after another, using domestic means to force compliance in domestic markets and using international pressures (economic, military, cultural) to do the same to other countries, cultures, and peoples.

The commodity form through which the subject enters the market place is not just through his or her "immaterial" labor, but through the appearance of one's self as unified semantic forms (i.e., as documents), within marketplaces. One presents images of one's self through social networks, one's romantic past is ranked and chatted about in social networks, one's recommendations are seen online, one's friends are known, one's life is valued through credit histories and the like, and if one teaches in academe then one's publications and teaching can be accessed and ranked online, as well. Social network databases are linked to and sold as the hosting corporation's property.

Today, these contribute to the documentary codes or "keys" that give one access and powers to institutional and social affordances, expressions, relationships, rights, and possibilities for wealth and happiness. In our present day, these "keys" that give one the privileges of other "keys"— other "doors" or opportunities—are remembered through social-technical information and communication systems that are sometimes interrelated through shared data, indexes, and search capabilities; one doesn't simply "have documents," increasingly a person *is* a set of varieties of documents, which constitute codes and passwords for powers of being and expression. Thus, the problem that individuals have today is that of not only managing, but of trying to prefigure their documentary codes in digital marketplaces, many of which have automated indexing systems that formally or socially prescreen both subjects and objects for documentary systems.

These economic and social commodity valuations of individuals as subjects and objects within advanced capitalist societies do not appear or function simply by symbol manipulations via algorithms. If this were the case, then these tokens would not have sense as social and cultural values, as well. Instead, these algorithmic manipulations must take place within, complement, and reinforce larger political economies of exchange of which they are a part. While there are certainly other economies functioning within the domain of those technologies and social relationships known as "the Internet," the capitalist economy and that of neoliberalism remains a driver of much of the popular use of the Internet and remains the "invisible hand" which overall attempts to drive its development both as a medium and as a set of infrastructural software and hardware technologies. Nonetheless, *the "gathering up" or sublimation of qualitative being, work, affects, and relationships into quantitative, algorithmic, devices often proves insufficient for addressing the ontological values of the former, whether this concerns friendship, understanding, or any other relationship that "takes time."*

Modeling

The problem of producing consistent representations across broad and various scales and across time ranges is a preoccupation of not just personal representation on the Internet, but in a different manner and concern, of information construction in the natural sciences as well. Paul N. Edwards (2010) has wonderfully shown the extent to which global climate science must rely on modeling, which involves not only the "cleansing" of text into data, but the "smoothing" out of aberrant data as well as the smoothing out of differences within and between different data types. The goal of climate science modeling is not only to show and compare past and present behaviors of the climate, but also to suggest possible future behaviors, and modeling is particularly important in cases such as climate science where experimentation is not possible or experimentation has only local values in terms of its subsequent evidential claims.

Epistemic problems regarding modeling in the social sciences can be more complex than with natural phenomena because models in the social sciences include within themselves the "mental models" that people and researchers have of themselves and of other people and their behaviors. Here, "smoothing" is not only performed by researchers in their reconciliation, modeling, and visualization of data, but by the subjects upon other subjects and upon themselves in their expressions and their identity formations. These choices both by researchers and by the subjects themselves may then further influence research, leading to reinforcing and self-reinforcing assumptions for research and research results.

The sociotechnical (self-)modeling of individuals and their (self-)positioning within political economies constitutes much of the state and commercial governance and construction of the subject in modernity. As a product of modern governance techniques, the modeling of the subject by bureaucratic and actuarial institutions and techniques reaches back to the eighteenth century and then continues not only through the state apparatus, but also through commercial sales and marketing. As JoAnne Yates (1989) has shown, in the nineteenth and twentieth centuries inventory assessment and sales reports gradually became managerial and predictive tools. These translated and eventually did away with narratives in sales reports, replacing narrative with numerical information and data that played the role of not only describing and reporting, but also predicting and shaping the needs of shop owners and consumers. Scientific management in modernity has brought together producers and consumers within just-in-time production and predictive marketing. Increasingly, the goal of a producer has been to systematize the entire production-consumption cycle.

As is well known, the rise of American empirical sociology evolved in part during the 1930s as a form of market and public opinion research in order to better predict and control consumer behavior. As the Keynesian consumptive- rather than production-driven economy took hold during the Great Depression and after, consumers had to be not only surveyed for desires and needs, but these desires and needs also needed to be shaped in order to be fulfilled within the limits of commodity production and its productive and distributive limits. Knowledge expressions were viewed by empirical sociologists as products of individual choices within a range of possible expressions as shown on surveys. Expression became understood as commodity choices, "free speech" being the equivalent of what people would choose to spend their money on within a range of options. This economy of "free speech" continues in the U.S. legal tradition, most recently with Supreme Court cases (*Citizens United v. Federal Election Commission*, 2010; *McCutcheon v. Federal Election Commission*, 2014) having to do with campaign contributions being treated as first amendment issues of free speech, except in this case—as consistent with the industrial economy and consumer economics more generally—the wealthy create the commodities (politicians, political parties, and political issues) which the populace then chooses from.

Mass and Crowd Psychology

As Ulus Baker (Baker 2001) argued, the ancient Greek notions of *episteme* and *doxa* are collapsed within a modern notion of opinion. The modern notion of opinion is not a product of argumentative, Socratic dialectic, but rather, it is that of an expression that fits within an aesthetics of opinions. One chooses an opinion out of a series of possible expressions as offered by broadly construed "information system," rather than arrives at an opinion through the rigor of argument or as a product of technical knowledge. In turn, such a notion of opinion comes to shape people's expressions, not least when the difference between knowledge and opinion collapses. Opinion becomes a choice of options within a market of delivered or retrievable goods. To "have" an opinion is to know something, foremost that of knowing something that others know something about or are curious about, and to know one's likes and dislikes in regard to such. In modernity, having an opinion is having or thinking that one has knowledge, which is related to being able to be informed about something and informing others about such; it fits within and is valued within systems of information exchange.

It is often said that newer technologies have surpassed the limits of modern production; that the consumer now drives production and that trends now measure real individual expressions rather than force individual expression within averages. It is assumed that we have advanced from a "mass" to a "crowd" psychology through social computing.

But from another perspective, the transition from early twentieth-century mass psychology to more contemporary crowd psychology may be seen dialectically. Whereas modern mass psychology and totalitarian politics subsumed individuals in a collective identity around the *imago* of the state or a leader as symbol of the state, crowd psychology involves taking alternating turns in leading, but still in a generally agreed upon direction. The singular is subsumed within the logic of the subject within the unfolding of an idea or concept, largely not as one disciplined by some other or others, but rather leading the idea to its fulfillment him- or herself. The subject is subjugated in mass psychology, but self-subsumed in crowd psychology as a participant and leader in a trend. This shift in the psychological and sociological conception of the individual, from the ideal of Western "existentialist" individualism to the "belonging" and teamwork of group psychology, is aided by the market pressures of neoliberal ideologies which demand individuality and innovative expressions but within the terms of market segments and social networks. Here, the self seeks external checks and balances in producing and consuming and being trained for such, seeing these *not as repressions to freedom, but rather, as affordances for freedom; not devices for the repression of personal powers, but codes for the possibility of expression and social and career advancement.* Education and acculturation become more permeated by goals and objectives, by correct and incorrect measures for teaching and for learning, for knowledge and ignorance, as compared to the previous existential model of psychology. Moral psychology, as well as individual knowledge and social affects, becomes permeated by neoliberal concerns for the self.

The "interiorization" (or what psychoanalysis calls the "introjection") of market norms into the self and person of individuals as a priori affordances and powers is what allows for neoliberal individualism and freedom and is what defines rational action today. The understanding of the self in terms of its powers for expressions in and by markets, rather than as powers outside of, prior to, and beyond markets, is what characterizes the socially adjusted, cultured, and educated contemporary individual. Through digital technology, such an individual fits within communicative networks that, directly or indirectly, lead to greater market production (whether those acts of production are immediately or later seen as profit making, for the producer or for others who are wealthier).

Ideological constraints for expression, communication, and identity are introjected into the self as "opportunities" for expression, communication, and identity. In post-Fordist production, for example, the worker who was subjugated within the disciplinary regime of the "vertical organization" (e.g., of the factory or the office space) has been, since the 1980s, "freed" within "flat structures" and "teams" and left to be more self-regulated at the workplace and in home offices. The logic of "the market" becomes introjected as the logic of the subject, not in its external *interpellation* or calling to the subject, but rather in the subject calling him- or herself as a voice of conscience (*these are my friends; this is what makes me happy; this is my job; this is to whom I belong; this is my identity, my opportunity, my way of connecting with others;* each event, each being and person, becomes declared with these demonstrative pronouns, as a statement, as evidence, as a document, as a naming and an inclusion and exclusion in relation to the world at large in relation to the I).

These post-Fordist rules and roles are passed down through cultural and repressive "apparatuses" (Althusser 2001) and means. The penalties for the lack of such rules in the raising of children, for example, are severe in a neoliberal economy that lacks a safety net and that has massive judicial and penitentiary systems and breeds the resentment of the middle class toward anyone that it sees as "not following the rules." Lacking such maturity, the child and then adult of those not in the ruling and leisure class may be severely disciplined by the marketplace and the courts until they "mature" or are simply marginalized outside of social and political existence. Today, ego ideals of motherhood and fatherhood, and for the children ego ideals of fear and guilt, run rampant across the media and in school, as signifiers of potential and potential failure or worse. The neoliberal screws have been pressed, extending to the destruction of childhood and the infantilizing of adulthood in anxieties for approval and success. "Excellence" must be, indeed, its own standard and reward, because it is the imaginary *Über-Ich* of neoliberal subsumption.

Social Big Data and Governmentality

Seen from the context of the modern documentary tradition, what are the norms that social big data imposes upon judgment—or what may be seen as the documentary emptying out of judgment—and how does such relate to what was known in the Enlightenment as freedom? This question is not just a contemporary one that has suddenly appeared, but one which has evolved alongside of and has intertwined with the neoliberal construction of subjectivity in modernity, not only with the statistical positioning of the subject within a market, but now, as a more predictive targeting and training of the subject, as one that is surveyed, tracked, and "targeted" as both an individual and as a member of a group, as both a producer and a consumer, as a citizen and as a non-citizen. No longer is the surveillance of the individual enough, but now he or she is co-located within predictive matrixes of actions and objects through linked associations with other subjects, objects, and events in databases and their indexes. Through this the subject is both disciplined by and afforded power.

The increased accuracy (or believed accuracy) of increased surveillance and feedback targeting through the collection of social big data and its analyses and social and political uses (ranging from drone predators to state surveillance in both democratic and communist/authoritarian governments to consumer targeting—for example, the targeting done by Target Corporation, as described in a 2012 *New York Times* article [Duhigg 2012])—belong to a conjoined mechanism of cybernetic *and* neoliberal governmentality, which crosses governmental and corporate databases and organizations. Social big data seeks to demarcate trends, which then directly or indirectly act as norms, which further consolidate individual and group action within market-determined norms (Rouvroy 2013). People are forced into competition, into a "freedom" that is monitored and checked within systems of feedback control. As Norbert Weiner suggested in the Cold War period (Wiener 1954, 1961), communicative control can be used toward a discourse of "rationality"; a rationality that is seen as proper to a given political economy. The documentary indexing of the subject provides the codes for the subject's social positioning and expressions by others and by itself. Thanks to networked, mobile devices, the subject can attempt to continuously propose him- or herself to the world as the subject of documentary representation.

The dominance of digital mediation for the overall social positioning and expressions of the subject gives rise to a regime of digital governance, which in its most textually reductive form follows the representations of data science. This science of data "facts" subsumes the former role of information and before that documentation. What distinguishes data science from information science and documentation as techniques of governance is the role of data modeling and the role that conjoined databases and regimes of data play in establishing empirical reality by simulacra. Such simulacra are the expressions of joined documentary subjects and objects as measured by variable parameters of political economy. As Antoinette Rouvroy writes:

Data, information, knowledge are thus more or less taken to be the same things. Such "knowledge" thus does not appear as a "production of the mind," with all the artificiality and cognitive and emotional biases unavoidably connoting mental productions, but as always already "given", immanent to the (digitally recorded) world, in which it is merely automatically "discovered", or from which it literally flourishes thanks to algorithmic operations rendering invisible correlations operational.... Knowledge is not produced *about* the world anymore, but *from* the digital world. A kind of knowledge that is not tested-by nor testing the world it describes and emanates from: algorithmic reality is formed inside the digital reality without any direct contact with the world it is aimed at representing. Rather than the validity of its predictive models, it is its operationality, its plasticity, its contribution to the "fluidification" of economic and social life (and thus of capitalism), its efficiency in sparing human agents time and efforts in the interpretation and evaluation of persons and events of the world that characterize the "intelligence" of "big data." (Rouvroy 2013, 147)

What distinguishes the rhetoric and epistemology of social big data from the uses of data before it? Rouvroy (2013) argues, first, that what is involved is the seeming transcendence of the need for not only judgment and interpretation, but also the need for empirical testing. (Indeed it is sometimes, strikingly, asserted by proponents of big data that hypotheses and "theory" emerge from the data, as if no discourse or concepts guided the tools of data gathering and interpretation—in other words, that big data not only brings about a state of pure positivist representation, but it does so beyond the need for scientific methods or for theory.[2]) There is a trust that the validation of models comes from other models, rather than from either empirical testing or from discursive consensus or historical interpretation, even when such are available. At the same time, the claims for knowledge are presented as immediate—"factual"—rather than as emergent through technologies, techniques, and methods, on the one hand, and interpreted through theory or a priori concepts, on the other hand.[3] *The data says ...; the data shows us...; we are only interested in data [not justifications/excuses/your opinion/your experience]...; big data and its mining and visualizations gives us a macroscopic view to see the world anew now*—these and similar phrases and tropes now fill the air with what is claimed to be a new form of knowledge and a new tool for governance that are superior to all others, past and present.

Social Big Data as Variable and Parametric Indexes

It is sometimes argued that the power of social big data collection and analysis lies most in predicting trends within which subjects are captured. One of the most distinguishing aspect of the state and commercial uses of social big data is they often involve a *variable* and *parametric* index that constantly monitors and *surveys* subjects and objects and their relationships in time. The indexes of social positioning are in this way "floating"; the measuring devices adjust to the relationships and their expressions, as well as can be shifted in order to show different perspectives.

This historical quality gives to social big data its quality of appearing to show and follow trends in the expressions of the spirit of an individual in his or her age, society, and culture. This historical quality, however, doesn't necessarily simply come from the data, but it can also come from indirect ideological and direct surveillance feedback mechanisms acting upon entities. The surveillance is done at the level of individuals, who are monitored and whose actions are predicted throughout key moments of their consumption or production, marking changes in trends and phase states, and recalculating the trajectory of entities according to these new parameters and relationships.

The individuals that are under surveillance may have various degrees of anonymity at first—the social, political, or institutional systems that track them have no real interest in them as singular selves other than as means to further increases and security in their own powers. Their status as selves is valuable only in so far as they are understood as calculable tendencies and nodes in networks, as threats or allies or sources of profit. Governing them takes the form of both limiting and affording choices toward what may be considered to be "productive" or useful expressions. The system attempts to predict and create needs and the fulfillment of needs, whether for potential shopping (Duhigg 2012), voting (Issenberg 2012), or any other intention. Rather than statistics being used to create the picture of an averaged individual, statistics are used to track individuals and aggregate them into predictions for behaviors for both singular individuals and groups, and in relation to objects.

The issue of governing the subject is that of the shaping of the will through information and communicative technologies so that it appears as rational expressions—as autonomous, yet as being part of group norms. Control is governance—creating markets of powers and expressions that come to constitute the expressions and identities of individuals and groups. At an ideological and metaphysical level, individual needs and their fulfillment gives *evidence* of "free choice" and the natural ontology of markets and empirical entities and relationships. Toward this, neoliberalist governance works to afford the possibility of needs and fulfillment *before* the subject's actions. It does this through promoting and trimming cultural forms and social norms, relying on the control of taste, opinion, and reason as formal parameters for prejudgment and therefore controlling the affordances for actions. If there are needs that aren't fulfilled or can't be filled, then they aren't needs, and are just the noise of malcontents, lunatics, or past ages.

The neoliberal documentary society is a society governed by means of collectively managed self-adaptation, afforded by documentary mediation. The individual is to serve and to save him- or herself through abundantly available and ubiquitous sociotechnical systems—automated calling trees, health care management systems, individual retirement account management, constant network connection through mobile devices, endless university diplomas and continual education, unbounded and endless work, online friendships, political participation in established parties, police-regulated protests, and so forth. Unlike the welfare state, the individuals are not averaged, but are given his or her "free will," one that is governed generally, though if necessary, concretely, point by point, by varieties of social constraints, interventions, and affordances, working as hidden and inaccessible strange attractors and surveillance and targeting systems. The documentary systems must be able to scan, identify, and predict general movements and particular expressions over time, and must be able to exert through feedback, and through their very shadow of real or imagined presences, control upon the subject. One is tracked as sets of relations and expressions *that give to the subject specific possibilities for actions and identity.* The function of neoliberal markets and documentary systems together as a mode of governance is to turn the *singularity* and *potentiality* of selves and texts into *individual* and *recognizable* expressions by means of diachronic and synchronic surveillance and control. *Governance using documentary systems must turn the potential into the possible, and so fit the person within logical systems of representation.*

The subject's "will" is increasingly shaped through informational and, in the sense of information theory, communicational, devices, networks, connections, and recognizable ends and goals. Google documentary indexes and analytics progress neatly to Google car because they both involve shaping the will—or what in psychoanalysis is called "the drive" (*Trieb*)— by communication networks. Whereas previously cars were advertised as extensions of the (traditionally symbolized, masculine) drive, soon the drive will be the product of informational and communicative relationships. Space becomes place, will becomes needs; *drive is mapped out and visualized* as intents and possibilities of communicative and information channels and their coded affordances for entrance, driving, and exiting. Physical maps are graphic displays of place points; the drive occurs between starting points and destination points, needs and possible objects. Once spaces become places, once places are documented by physical coordinates, then destinations and starting points can be linked by means of possible routes and—increasingly, especially when constantly updated via sensors and user feedback—as predictable and updatable times of travel. These coordinates can then be given names or other identifying symbols through the intermediaries of gazetteers or other documentary indexes and so can take on social and cultural, historical and political, values, as well.

In social big data we are not just documentary subjects, not just documentary objects, but rather we are the two conjoined with each other as parametrically viewed historical expressions. This is to say that practically speaking, politically and socially, we *are*, and don't just participate as, these conjoined subjects and objects. Today, we are drivers between places in certain types of vehicles on crowded roads with time limits and expectations, not just persons "out for a drive" as used to be said; we are consumers of commodities with commodity needs and brands, not just users of things; we are students becoming trained in something, not just persons interested in experiencing or even becoming knowledgeable; we are "moms" and "tiger moms," with enormous social and personal role expectations and ideal narratives placed upon adults and children. Social big data conjoins subjects and subjects and subjects and objects with each other according to algorithms of need (Thomas 2012). They help fulfill *our* needs and they extend *my* needs. Our places, searches, expressions, and actions more generally are indexed, and then these indexes are re-injected back into social and documentary systems, which readjust themselves for further predictable expressions. And today, we are products of not even whole documents, as they were once known, but rather of documentary fragments and representations—"information"—in communication with each other and in communication with ourselves. Ultimately, we are mediated by sociotechnical documentary indexes that index each of us to performances within political economies, as evidence or not of the idea (and therefore value) of being for those systems, and then this evidence assures codes for further possibilities of performances and being. Like stocks, our "future performances" are not guaranteed, and so both market and state surveillance are necessary for the system as a whole to have the full faith and credit of both the governors and the governed.

Reading "Big Information"

In this chapter I have been discussing social big data as constituting a form of documentary governmentality. Data, as Antoinette Rouvroy (2013) argues, is often understood as an auto-affective entity that, like earlier uses of "information" and "knowledge," is understood as self-evident facts. In big data, machine algorithms process and index data relationships, often over time. Out of such relationships, the documentary expressions of subjects and objects are seen to emerge.

As we saw in the beginning of this book, the discourse on the necessity of information processing for information overload goes at least as far back as the end of the nineteenth century and early twentieth, and one response to it was Paul Otlet's description of skimming as the privileged mode of reading. Today, as well, skimming is a manner of cognitively "processing" texts by looking for knowledge patterns and meanings that correspond to the subject's information needs.

To end this chapter, then, I would like to move back from "big data" per se, and discuss what we might call "big information," by which I mean encounters with large sets of documents and the act of reading as skimming that we bring to this. As I will argue in this final section, the political economy of neoliberalism—gathering within it a cultural understanding of modernity as efficiency in production—comes to bear upon the nature of reading, time, and, as we will return to in the conclusion of this book, upon the possibility or impossibility of critique. Beginning with documentation theory and practice in the end of the nineteenth and the beginning of the twentieth centuries and continuing into today, in the modern documentary tradition the subject's practice of reading becomes increasingly instrumental, surveying texts and persons (and beings more generally) toward their ability to answer the subject's information needs in efficient and timely manners. Thus, as we saw discussed earlier in this book in the passage from Paul Otlet, reading changes from being a hermeneutic activity of "close" and "critical reading" to being an instrumental activity of skimming. Information retrieval and other documentary techniques, technologies, and methods are utilized to help make skimming possible and to increase the relevancy of the document sets to the subject's information needs. The skills of using documentary techniques, technologies, and methods, and of skimming materials toward answering information needs are often called today "information literacy" skills. The contexts for information literacy skills are generally productivist and, particularly, task-oriented, but may be for entertainment and leisure ends as well.

The extension of information literacy to practices of reading is an extension of the notion of information to texts. "Information literacy" as a broad concept in regard to readings and texts is thus a sociotechnical practice of reading via the use of modern documentary techniques and technologies toward the answering of information needs, which as I have argued, are prefigured by both ideological and technical documentary devices and parameters.

Nathaniel F. Enright has written on the confluence of information literacy and neoliberalism in the context of higher education reform "whose major purpose is the functional training of the labor force in line with the needs of capital" (Enright 2013). Understanding information literacy from the aspect of browsing and skimming information toward the goal of increasing one's market value (or as the economist Gary Becker might put it, increasing one's "human capital"), Enright writes:

> The argument that I wish to finally advance here is not only that the information literate is the neoliberal subject *par excellence* but is also structured around the notion of human as *homo economicus*. Indeed, in all of the policy [i.e., Australian education policy, which Enright analyzes] the information literate is always conceptualized as a rational, self-interested individual who can recognize "the need for information" and continually "re-evaluates the nature and extent of the information need." It really is as if [Gary] Becker's calculation that "all human behavior can be viewed as involving participants who maximize their utility from a stable set of preferences and accumulate an optimal amount of information and other inputs in a variety of markets" has come to pass. (Enright 2013, 32–33)

Katherine Hayles's discussion of "hyper" or "surface" reading in her recent book, *How We Think: Digital Media and Contemporary Technogenesis* (Hayles 2012), is one resource in which to examine reading as a practice of information literacy. As of this writing, Hayles is a professor and director of graduate studies in literature at Duke University, and a well-known and respected scholar in humanities readings of contemporary information and communication technologies. In her book Hayles argues for new methods and techniques of reading, particularly in student instruction and in research in the humanities. She discusses what she terms "hyper reading" and "machine reading," specifically against the background of the tradition of "close reading" in the humanities, and especially there in academic English departments. Referring to John Guillory's work on archival research, Hayles stresses the role of "scanning" and "skimming" in "hyper reading":

> As a strategic response to an information-intensive environment, hyper reading is not without precedent. John Guillory, in "How Scholars Read" (2008), notes that "the fact of quantity is an intractable empirical given that must be managed by a determined method if analysis or interpretation is to be undertaken." He is not talking here about digital reading but about archival research that requires a scholar to move

through a great deal of material quickly to find the relevant texts or passages. He identifies two techniques in particular, scanning (looking for a particular keyword, image, or other textual feature) and skimming (trying to get the gist quickly). He also mentions the book wheel, a physical device invented in the Renaissance to cope with the information explosion when the number of books increased exponentially with the advent of print. Resembling a five-foot-high wheel, the book wheel held several books on different shelves and could be spun around to make different texts accessible, in a predigital print version of hyper reading. (Hayles 2012, 61–62)

Hayles's (2012) claims regarding "hyper reading" may remind us of Otlet's claim that we discussed at the beginning of the book, namely, that we have entered a new age of reading texts and people: skimming. Hayles claims that hyper reading and computer-aided indexes and other digitally mediated tools for quantitative humanities work are necessary tools for addressing massive amounts of information, and that such tools are needed given what she claims are students' impatience with close reading.

Despite the use of scientific nomenclature, such as "methods" and "techniques," when describing reading and writing in the humanities, rhetorical approaches tend to be rather heterogeneous. Browsing, scanning, and skimming were always done in various stages of humanities research, though especially in the early stages. The difference, compared with Hayles's argument, is that they were never valorized as being reading itself or taken as being the main source for the value of humanities research. Why then this reversal of values for what were, previously, seen as preliminary acts to a "deeper" sense of reading?

As we have discussed, one reason is the claim that the student is faced with problems of information overload. This leads to information literacy-like claims for methods, techniques, and technologies that might help the student find and evaluate information for information needs. The second reason, however, has to do with Hayles's claims that students and the English profession are tired of "close reading." The purpose of her chapter and book are to advocate for something after this.

According to Hayles, close reading has become a unifying method for approaching texts generally in English departments (2012, 57–59). She particularly focuses upon one of what she calls the "dominant" techniques of "close reading," namely, "symptomatic reading," which she traces to, for example, Frederic Jameson's ideological critique of textual production: "For Jameson, with his motto 'Always historicize,' the text is an alibi for subtextual ideological formations" (Hayles 2012, 59). For Hayles, the technique of "symptomatic reading" has outlived its usefulness: "After more than two decades of symptomatic reading, however, many literary scholars are not finding it a productive practice, perhaps because (like many deconstructive readings) its results have begun to seem formulaic, leading to predictable conclusions rather than compelling insights" (Hayles 2012, 59). Returning to a special issue of the New Historicism journal *Representations* in 2009 ("The Way We Read Now") Hayles concludes:

In a paraphrase of Gilles Deleuze and Félix Guattari's famous remark, "We are tired of trees," the *Representations* special issue may be summarized as, "We are tired of symptomatic reading." The issue's contributors are not the only ones who feel this way. In panel after panel at the conference sponsored by the National Humanities Center in spring 2010 entitled "The State and Stakes of Literary Studies," presenters expressed similar views and urged a variety of other reading modes, including "surface reading," in which the text is examined not for hidden clues, but its overt messages; reading aimed at appreciation and articulation of the text's aesthetic value; and a variety of other reading strategies focusing on affect, pleasure, and cultural value. (Hayles 2012, 59)

While "close reading" in some senses has roots in English departments and New Criticism, "symptomatic readings" are much broader in origin. "Symptomatic reading" is sort of a pejorative code word in literary studies for broadly understood, "deconstructive" readings, including shared Marxist oriented engagements, which attempt to outline the "ideologemes" (Jameson 1982) that are circulated and reproduced in textual expressions. The notion of "symptom" here is related to deconstruction's appropriation of it from psychoanalysis, as the notion of an irreducible sign that is worked out in the unfolding of the text by forces both beyond, and functioning within, the text proper—and whose trace is often relegated to marginal status or is dismissed in the expression of the text's "information" or content proper (its "presence"). Deconstruction as a type of reading is an unwrapping of the play of forces and power that produce a text's "content," "meaning," or what we may call its "information."

"Symptomatic readings" are sometimes taken as part of a "hermeneutics of suspicion," in so far as they start from the assumption that the meaning of texts is not self-generated and that the task of scholarly reading is to try and understand how meaning is produced in a text and what the function of texts are in different contexts of reading. Textual meaning is a symptom of reading, and reading is a hermeneutic and socioculturally constructed activity. The content or information of a text is a product of the stabilization of the meaning of signifiers by other signifiers, and so there is not a definitive "outside" to the text, just as there is not a definitive "inside" or content within the text prior to reading. Meaning is not auto-affectively produced, but instead, its evidentiality or "information" is due to plays of forces and systems of stabilization that the author attempts to control, but which, by definition, exceed the control of the author. The common thread in this "hermeneutics of suspicion" (commonly said to reach back to Freud, Nietzsche, and Marx) is the problem of Kant's critical philosophy, namely, that of trying to account for the production and reproduction of "presences" and their repetition or "representations." How is the "empirical," that is, what appears to be existent, brought into the understanding? How does a stable meaning in a text appear to readers and what in and outside of a text proper must be privileged and suppressed in order to get this meaning to appear and be conveyed to the reader in a clear and distinct manner?

In sum, English department "close readings" and "symptomatic readings" have their origin in functionalist-social accounts of the production of meaning and understanding and the appearance of subjects and objects as the products or the "content" of social, cultural, and political forces operating in texts and beyond. These reading practices are part of a critical tradition reaching back to Kant's critical philosophy and its Enlightenment context. And it is for this reason that what in the 1970s and 1980s was known as "theory" (i.e., "critical theory," broadly understood) crossed many different disciplines (including English), and it is also for this reason that contemporary English department research now extends to many non-literary textual research projects. The notion of the text is not just literary, nor can it be confined to documents. All texts are rhetorical products and so utilize various devices for persuasion, some of which may be more used in literature, though not exclusively. In sum, "deep reading" (i.e., critique) can hardly be said to have originated or to have ended in Anglo-American English departments in the twentieth and now the twenty-first centuries.

Hayles's (2012) account of student and professional "tiredness" with reading texts as material and social production, and her valorization of skimming, pleasure reading, and "cultural value," could be read as a politically conservative celebration of a return to cultural values and literacy-skills education in English and other humanities departments. (New Criticism was a reaction to earlier historical research and literature appreciation in

English departments.) And though it is clearly not Hayles's intent in her text (2012), the cultural rejection of close and critical readings and a celebration of aesthetic pleasure and beauty in its place could remind one of the celebrations of aestheticism in German and Italian fascism during the early twentieth century, when critical formalism and the works of the avant-garde were rejected and suppressed in light of what was supposed to be popular cultural pleasures and beautiful form.

It is, perhaps, understandable that theory may have become "tiring" when the original theoretical texts (and the sources that they critique and comment on) have ceased being closely read themselves and instead have been substituted for by informational handbooks, introductions, "idiot guides," and other documentary reductions and abstractions, which serve as interpretative devices for "critical methods" in analyzing the mainstays of the English department canon (literary period and genre studies). It isn't surprising that the very texts that descriptively and prescriptively demand a *time of reading* have passed out of popularity because of the overall political economy of time within which they have been inserted, namely an economy of time where they are seen (as per Otlet) as consumptive of, or simply a waste of, time, other than in a summary form that reduces them to tools of "method" for more canonical production.

In short, Hayles's (2012) celebration of aestheticism and skimming and her criticism of critique could be read as a celebration of the values of a political culture of documentary representation and production, particularly in an age of ubiquitous digital devices and mobile entertainment, where critical work takes time from what could be otherwise be spent in more entertaining or productive manners for students. What it criticizes is reading as an activity that draws the reader in toward changing the notion and experience of time in a production- and entertainment-oriented world. From a certain perspective, it criticizes *literature* (broadly understood as texts qua hermeneutic inscriptions), and it valorizes whatever writing forms appear as *documents* (that is, texts qua topics or "aboutness" which correspond to likely information needs). From this perspective, it is somewhat paradoxical and puzzling that even as Hayles celebrates recent tools for the documentary treatment of texts, she then finds the products of tools for the documentary treatment of theoretical texts to be tiring and predictable. In short, as Suzanne Briet (2006) suggested happens with new technologies, Hayles's celebration of new digital technologies of reading seems to be a celebration of the new social rhythms introduced by these technologies; the celebration of an attention economy and "multitasking," introduced by the ubiquitous presence of digital mediation and entertainment into everyday life, along with the pressures of neoliberalism.

What we seem to have then in Hayles's celebration of "surface" or "hyper" reading is a celebration of ideological reproduction and a positive endorsement of the text's role in this through representation, as a source for confirming the self's own social and cultural inscriptions through the individual's experience of aesthetic harmony or pleasure. It is a celebration of the subject's recognition in the texts of the subject's own tastes and needs. It stands in distinction to critical theory's attempt to understand the forces that create taste and need, and indeed, that lead to subjectivity. "Surface" or "hyper" reading is a reading through representational mediation.

In contrast, it may be suggested that an aesthetics of representation—whether such occurs in the media, or in reading as skimming, or with classification, metadata, and visualization techniques, or even in the practices of science as a posteriori method—*needs* critical theory and deep reading; not as a modern sense of information, but as counter-information. Critical theory intervenes in our customs of thought and practices, in our use of representations, in order to raise issues about power, production, representation, judgment, justice, and the direction of society and culture generally. Critical theory provides a necessary and critical contrary—a deep reading—to the surface readings that we routinely do in our everyday lives. One deploys critical theory not in order to reproduce the already popular ideological order, but in order to engage and try to understand, and if necessary critique, it.

7 Conclusion: The Modern Documentary Tradition and the Site and Time of Critique

I return here to our final discussion in the previous chapter on the topic of contemporary documentary mediated reading, which, as we saw in the very beginning of this book, was valorized in the tradition of European documentation by Paul Otlet at the start of the twentieth century. The imperative for the modern tradition of critical theory and later readings of "symptoms" did not originate in English departments or in any academic specialization, but from Enlightenment thought. In library science, the tradition that emanates from this imperative is called "intellectual freedom," that is, freedom of access to expressions and a person's rights to free expressions, which are seen as intrinsic rights of human beings as communicative and mentally complex beings. Hayles (2012) may be correct that many faculty and students in English departments are tired of formulaic critical methods as applied to literary and other texts in the field. Nevertheless, critique of a priori assumptions (and of a posteriori applications of conceptual assumptions) in method and technique is an often marginalized and missing element of scientific and scholarly research and writing, and as well in ordinary practical activities. The formal modes of scientific rhetoric in publication and presentation often excludes critical a priori analyses. This may lead researchers to believe that further research along given founding conceptual assumptions is actually investigating real phenomena or producing fruitful research, whereas the research is merely showing taxonomically and methodologically operationalized impositions of a priori assumptions upon empirically designated research subjects and objects. And likewise in everyday life, as it was once common to say, custom seduces us all, and so hides the social and cultural devices and powers that make up the ordinary expressions and understandings of our lives and interactions.

The modern university as it has appeared in the West and as it has spread throughout the rest of the world may be traced back to Wilhelm von Humboldt's vision for the University of Berlin, founded in 1810, which saw education as made up of technical innovation and critique, both being necessary in service to the state. The modern technocratic university since World War II has more and more marginalized critique, first from the sciences and more recently from many areas of the humanities where it has been replaced by a return to values education and skills training, both within the context of a privatization in funding and a greater consumerist and job training orientation in universities. Indeed, throughout the university and throughout contemporary society, critique has often been replaced by information, opinion, and scientific method. But, more data and more techniques and method can't by themselves solve the problem of poor or unseen conceptual foundations, nor do such "mores" address ideological and economic curbs upon what type of information and communication are practically allowed both in teaching and research.

The concept of critique doesn't originate in postmodernism or any other contemporary movement or cultural genre. Kant's famous three critiques in the spheres of *cognitive* knowledge, *practical* knowledge ("moral" knowledge in eighteenth-century parlance), and *taste* are part of a larger argument against both metaphysical and empirical dogmatisms, and they are part of a larger project of Enlightenment thought which can be glimpsed in Kant's well-known publication of December 1784 in the journal, *Berlinische Monatsschrift*, "An Answer to the Question: What is Enlightenment?" (Kant 2009). In this article, critique is viewed as necessary for social progress and is seen as an intrinsic right and property of being human. Human beings have a right to intervene in the political economy and times in which they find themselves living. Complex and innovative expressions, and therefore "thought," are a right granted by their very types of existence. And their existence is one where the meaning of time is a concern and an opportunity for social and personal reinvention; it is not just a given. In Kant's text (2009), enlightenment is an event, both personally and socially. The demand for it is an intrinsic property of human existence, which each person carries within him or herself.

Skimming allows for a turning away from the challenge of the text or the other person toward the self. One skims for what one already more or less knows, for what one is expecting. The documentary friend is consulted, and responses are browsed to answer the questioner's information needs, which themselves are often tied to production and entertainment markets of selling and buying labor, information, and other goods. As a practice of reading, skimming is a product of an age that demands increased production by students and by faculty within an economy of both overproduction and competition for scarce monetary and temporal resources, a personal and professional life made up of extremes of competition and diversion, and the increasing replacements of human beings by computer and computer-aided devices. Texts that are picked up, read-to-hand, and easily incorporated within social and professional productivity and everyday learning and entertainment are valorized and, in turn, written and published.

Today, it sometimes seems that reading books wastes too much time and so they are marked into fragments by indexes and they come to be made up of articles by different authors. Keywords are used to find parts of texts and the texts or these parts are gathered into "infographic" representations. Articles waste too much time, and so are abstracted and summarized and their results charted. These waste too much time and so we read web "long journalism" and short fragments of web articles. These waste too much time, and so we inform and communicate through commentary fragments and "like" indicators on Facebook. These waste too much time and so we use Twitter. These waste too much time, and so we simply photograph our experiences and post them on Instagram or the like. The documentary universe enlarges, the attention economy becomes shorter and shorter, and the demands of reading become less and less.

Despite broader information and communication capabilities, political and everyday life has become in some manners more narcissistic, not less, than before the Internet. We seek what we more or less already know, we ignore one another by staying glued to our devices, and we make and break relationships by the mediation of algorithms and indexes. Where children of the 1960s wished that they could take their televisions with them everywhere, including to school, now we can. Here one sees the sometimes familiar outlines of the paradox of the psychopathology of modern technological information and communication technologies: new technologies are invented to overcome the fragmentation and alienation of modern capitalist life and then end up in some ways increasing this fragmentation and alienation in the most essential areas of life.

It is often forgotten that the practice of book indexing became more common, particularly within Anglo-American books, only in the mid-twentieth century. As Paul Otlet's works suggest, indexing and other such documentary techniques that have turned into broad sociotechnical mediations are products of a political economy of rapid technologies and limited time and attention.[1]

The modern documentary age, made up of documentation, information science, and data and their sciences, is an age that valorizes these "information types" as a type of human or machine ready-to-hand knowledge. Their representational qualities "save time" and condense intellectual space. Psychologically, they intensify the modern experience of time in moods such as anxiety and boredom (Heidegger 1962); boredom is dreaded and anxiety is fetishized in information overload, overstimulation, multitasking, and eventually, consequential mental exhaustion and collapse (Berardi 2001) as a sign of commitment and maturity to productive institutions and to the preservation of the self. Anxiety is further created through entertainment and recreational devices so as to create a modicum of challenge in response to the relatively uncontrollable anxieties stemming from unbearable economic and corrupt political systems and an apocalyptic environmental reality. Like the mastery of wish fulfillment in dreams, and like the uses of earlier media such as film (Benjamin 1968), capital orients both technological innovation and self-development toward those devices and abilities that promise the virtual conquering of the rhythms and violence of reality through their simulacra. Video games allow children to master simulated traumas, rather than address real personal, social, and planetary problems collectively. They largely reproduce the bourgeois sense of personal crisis and the need to individually conquer such, rather than addressing the need for collective action. Though parents scream and yell about their children being on video games, the games are perfect mirrors of their own anxieties and methods of control and expression, most being equally fanciful and equally useless against the larger issues that determine lives.

The contemporary sense of time in moods is fixated upon objects of seeming production and entertainment so that the moods (and time) disappear in obsessive-compulsive narcissistic drives and distal devices. A sense of community and being based on an experience of being and time as finitude is lost in a sense of community as endless production, pointless triumphs, and the need to always produce more of these. Death, and with this, life itself has become simply an item of information, to be consumed and produced, and so, in our age of economic and ecological collapse, in Walter Benjamin's words that end his famous essay, "The Work of Art in the Age of Mechanical Reproduction" (1936): "[human being's] self-alienation has reached such a degree that it can experience its own destruction as an aesthetic pleasure of the first order" (Benjamin 1968, 242).

We exist online in virtual worlds of endless handshakes and endless tasks, the panacea to our wanting to be together but being unwilling or unable to, and to the fragmented and disjoined residues of loves, friends, and texts. We experience both the desire for others and the melancholy of non-fulfillment, documented. Our games give us a mastery of fantastic universes, while the crumbling of ourselves, our friends, our society, and the relatively (geologically speaking) recent ecology of the planet itself remain the real challenges that we feel powerless to address and often even acknowledge or recognize. We text and email our neighbors, lovers, and coworkers sitting next door or across the room from us. We play games, text, and answer emails as others surround and talk to us, and we hang on our mobile phones. We assume that large-scale data and its analytics will solve the environmental and social problems of our too-large consumption and will manage the scale of our outpaced production by yet more production. We train the young to become information technologists for the very types of technologies that are putting them out of work and creating permanent un- and underemployment and the "end of work." In short, we trust new forms of information and knowledge technologies to solve the very problems of our lives that they cannot or that they sometimes lead to.

By means of documentary abstraction and their technological-social manipulations as heuristics of social, economic, and psychological assumptions, documentation and its offspring, as Suzanne Briet (1951) wrote, represent and lead the way in a modernity characterized by rhythms of "efficiency" and a dream of *endless production*. As Antoinette Rouvroy writes in reflecting upon her own article: "Formulated as an inquiry about the state of knowledge, power and subjects after the computational turn, it turns out as a reformulation of the question of the possibility of critique, recalcitrance and subjectivation in an epistemic and political universe gradually deserted by empirical experiment and deductive, causal logic, and with regard to a mode of government appearing to disregard the reflexive and discursive capabilities (as well as their 'moral capabilities') of human agents, in favor of the computational, pre-emptive, context- and behavior-sensitive management of risks and opportunities" (Rouvroy 2013, 144).

Against recalcitrance, reflection, hesitancy, and silence, the ideology of the modern documentary age gives us products, production, efficiency, and the attention economy; against poetic *techne* it gives us the technologically completed and reproduced; against problematics, questions, and judgments it promises the certitude of documents, information, and data as exact answers; against lived experience it poses accumulated data and a posteriori method and technologically mediated facts and entertainment; against performances it poses representations (but in the appearance of being auto-affective presences or "facts"); against one's own solicitude and concern for others as the fellow being that one is, it poses others as "information resources" for one's own advancement in political economy and its institutions; against the *respons*ibility of personal judgment it poses the preemption of judgment by computationally and other technologically/technically mediated results; against critical thought and situational judgment it poses the aesthetics of formulaic reasoning and pronouncements and, indeed, entertainment; against literature it poses documentary "facts" through documentation, information, data, and their sciences; against singular education it poses mass instruction; and against language, dialogue, and the performance of inscription it poses standards of clarity and certainty within privileged economies of representation. In short, as I pointed out in my earlier book (Day 2001), the ideology and rhetoric of the age of the modern documentary tradition ("the information age" and its society) promises cheery days for all, if we would just accept the information present and future that we are told is true and not look beyond or outside of this.

As Heidegger argued, however, the culture of "efficiency" and "productiveness" in technological modernity has the psychological affect of suppressing the experience of *finitude* as a central concern of human beings with time. It masks the foundational ontological relationships of *Mitsein* that relate each *Dasein* to one another and to other beings. It does this by exploiting fundamental manners of being human and directing these toward production and profit. (While so much human value has been and is being produced by free labor on the Internet, there is no social mechanism, such as a social wage, to reward this and to continue it, and instead, as usual in capitalism, the owners of capital profit from human beings' fundamental concern with one another and increase their profits by using and reusing human concern for capital concerns, being and beings for profit.)

In Otlet and Briet's works—as in the history of the *science* of documentation, information, and data in the twentieth century and now the twenty-first—little *critical* reflection upon information or documentation as a cultural, social, or political symptom occurs; this is not only because both Otlet and Briet were professional advocates of documentation, but intrinsically because such a "symptomatic" reading is at odds with our modern understandings of documentation, information, and now data as privileged, and indeed sometimes, as the only form, of knowledge and experience, and so as the governing mediator for understanding and actions. In such an episteme, at least when it expands to having a total reach upon society and our life-spheres, *critique* finds it difficult to gain a foothold for reevaluating normative values or raising other values, not least that of non-instrumental values for being and being with one another.

We could say that it is not the technologies "themselves" that are the issue, but rather their unfolding under dominating political economies and metaphysical concepts that reduce their potentialities. In a sense this seems true, but on the other hand, there are no such things as technologies "themselves." All technologies are sociocultural assemblages and quite often there are mixtures of potential politics in their design. The history of the twentieth century shows that modern information and communication technologies emerge, are celebrated for their new temporalities, their new ability to refocus our attention, and their new social possibilities, but before too long they are remediated into reproducing the dominant politics and economies, and their liberating possibilities quickly begin to be lost. The vast hopes for social movements that the Internet promised only twenty years ago or less are quickly being lost to personal isolation, capitalist markets, and industry and government surveillance. The Internet has brought a world of knowledge and learning to people who can access it that was simply impossible to imagine even twenty-five years ago. But without critique, including critique of the popular and professional rhetoric of the digital age, this could be lost. Like Walter Benjamin's notes on the Paris arcades or passages, we are already beginning to look back at the shimmering artifact of digital culture that once promised the paradises of its age. And this looking back and being disappointed comes increasingly quickly in regard to the most recent hopes of digital culture these days.

It is difficult to believe that in the midst of so many problems today that critique is not needed. The Enlightenment critique may be specific and often paradoxical in its own historical contexts, but critique as such is common and necessary for any society or person that seeks meaning and value in life. Without critique, the right of people and persons to invent and reinvent their own lives and to make their own experiences disappears, not only as a right, but also as the essence of being human. Critique is an event that attempts to alter social and personal indexes and how they are composed, accounted for, and valued.

The problem of critique, in the midst of the modern documentary episteme and its modes of representation, extends not just to "the human" but more importantly beyond this, it extends to all beings in their singularity. The fundamental importance of the problem of being appears even more strongly in the face of the historicism of what is popularly called and assumed to be "the information age" and the "information society," because in such a modern conception of information the very notion of critique is marginalized.

Critically viewed, what burns most clearly from the edges and fractures of the modern documentary episteme are not documents, information, and data and their modern values, but that which withdraws from these; indeed, that which is beaten back by these appearances: the materiality of beings and texts. Texts are what the great documentary institutions have collected, whether they act as evidence or not. Their arrangement and organization were not meant as reductions of the texts, nor were all the texts meant to be evidential of "facts." Just like the singularity of persons and all beings, these are to be valued not simply for the construction and preservation of a civilization, but beyond this, for their *reading,* and in this, their *reinvention and renewal* of such. And for this reason both texts and beings cannot be typed and stay the same. The type and the singular are different; they cannot be dialectically collapsed into a single idea.

(And for this reason, this book has inverted the story of historical consciousness in our day, not in order to show it as natural, but rather to show it as real, by stressing its strongest forms, its sciences and their presences throughout our lives, in other words, its "rationality." However, what is shown as real must be read, and so in this methodological inversion of ideology its constituent forms, including its technologies, are given to rereading and reinscription. There is nothing natural, or in this sense "real," about historical consciousness, other than its reality as the rational; but this can be contested—however difficult that may be in word or deed—because it is for us so rational, so much of our consciousness and being.)

Critically viewed, even in the moment of the strongest appearance of a metaphysical concept in its concrete manifestations—that is, in its "science" or "sciences," its "factuality," and its empirical "reasonableness"— there remains the fragility of its entities and the logic and the devices for its appearances. In the symptom of an historical over-determination—either in a society or in an individual—there exists the pathology of its composition and appearance, and its presence and privileges, but also the fragments of other promises.

In the mirror of such determinations—in the mirror of what are called the "information age" and its "society," of what I have called the "modern documentary tradition"—there appears in its fractures and edges the singularity of beings and their expressions. Not as predictable moments, nor as types, nor even as functions of either habits or trends, but as radical expressions of life that can change all these, reimagine them, and begin again. These are the "remainders" of our modern sense of information, informing us of our being. They don't and won't disappear no matter the violence that they may suffer from the ideas, tropes, or evidence of representational governance.

The historical form of the modern documentary tradition may continue to socially advance, and yet each generation of such doesn't advance purely, but with the entanglements of what it tries to leave behind. This remainder is what critique attempts to keep free from any single concept of being, and which it attempts to liberate from such a concept to begin with.

What most informs us about our modern sense of "information" is what gives rise to it and remains. Only from this can "information," and with it, all sorts of documents and the modern documentary tradition itself, be seen as having living value or detracting from living value. We need to hear what "information" says, what informs it, and what informs us otherwise. What we *take* (in both a positive and a negative sense) from what we call "information" today must not only be information, but even more importantly, something other, namely, understanding. And to do this, we must begin to understand how we are indexically mediated as modern documentary beings.

Notes

Preface

1. When I was an undergraduate in philosophy, a visiting lecturer once told us a joke that there were two kinds of skeptics in this world: an East Coast skeptic and a West Coast skeptic. They both see roughly the same thing, but the first dwells on it and the second one forgets about it and goes surfing. Like all jokes, it deals with stereotypes; people live in many differing situations on both coasts (for example, the economic, social, and cultural distance between Palo Alto and East Palo Alto is quite large). I must confess, however, that where I live, and so this book, is closer to the "East Coast" in this joke.

Chapter 1

1. So, for example, we come to fulfill an information need in a library or other setting by finding out what is available, and so, we arrive at the "real need" only through the process of browsing, trying, and choosing. The library science literature is filled with theories that suggest a patron's "real need" is something hidden in his or her mind or lost in the patron's nervousness when confronted by information institutions or professionals, but this is silly. In an uncertain environment, we discover what we need by investigating what that environment has to offer, and then we accept something that seems right as being what we want or, retroactively, as what we wanted in the first place.

2. "De tout temps la latinité et son héritage ont donné au mot *document* le sens d'enseignement ou de preuve. Le dictionnaire de RICHELET, comme celui de LITTRÉ en apportent deux témoignages français. Une bibliographe contemporaine soucieuse de clarté a lancé cette brève définition: « Un document est une preuve à l'appui d'un fait ».

Si l'on se réfère aux définitions « officielles » de l'Union Française des Organismes de Documentation [2], on constate que le document est présenté ainsi: « toute base de connaissance fixée matériellement et susceptible d'être utilisée pour consultation, étude ou preuve ».

Cette définition a été parfois mise en échec par des linguistes ou par des philosophes, épris comme il se doit de minutie et de logique. Grâce à leur analyze du contenu de la notion, on a pu proposer ici une définition, la plus approchée qui soit à l'heure actuelle, mais aussi la plus abstraite, et partant, la moins accessible: « tout indice concret ou symbolique, conservé ou enregistré, aux fins de représenter, de reconstituer ou de prouver un phénomène ou physique ou intellectuel ».

Une étoile est-elle un document ? Un galet roulé par un torrent est-il un document ? Un animal vivant est-il un document ? Non. Mais sont des documents les photographies et les catalogs d'étoiles, les pierres d'un musée de minéralogie, les animaux catalogués et exposés dans un Zoo.

A notre époque de transmissions multipliées et accélérées, le moindre évènement, ou scientifique ou politique, lorsqu'il a été porté à la connaissance du public, s'alourdit aussitôt d'une « vêture de documents » (Raymond BAYER). Admirons la fertilité documentaire d'un simple fait de départ: par exemple, une antilope d'une espèce nouvelle a été rencontrée en Afrique par un explorateur qui a réussi à en capturer un individu qu'il ramène en Europe pour notre Jardin des Plantes. Une information de presse fait connaître l'évènement par des communiqués de journaux, de radio, par les actualités cinématographiques. La découverte fait l'objet d'une communication à l'Académie des Sciences. Un professeur du Muséum en fait état dans son enseignement. L'animal vivant est mis en cage et catalogué (jardin zoologique). Une fois mort il sera empaillé et conservé (au Muséum). Il est prêté à une Exposition. Il passe en sonorisé au cinéma. Son cri est enregistré sur disque. La première monographie sert à établir partie d'un traité avec planches, puis une encyclopédie spéciale (zoologique), puis une encyclopédie générale. Les ouvrages sont catalogués dans une bibliothèque, après avoir été annoncés en librairie (catalogs d'éditeurs et Bibliographie de la France). Les documents sont recopiés (dessins, aquarelles, tableaux, statues, photos, films, microfilms), puis sélectionnés, analysés, décrits, traduits (productions documentaires). Les documents se rapportant à cet évènement sont l'objet d'un classement scientifique (faune) et d'un classement idéologique (classification). Leur conservation enfin et leur utilization sont déterminées par des techniques générales et par des méthodes valables pour l'ensemble des documents, méthodes étudiées en associations nationales et en Congrès internationaux.

L'antilope cataloguée est un document initial et les autres documents sont des documents seconds ou dérivés."

(Many thanks to Laurent Martinet for posting the original of Suzanne Briet's *Qu'est-ce que la documentation* on the Internet; retrieved from: http://martinetl.free.fr/suzannebriet/questcequeladocumentation).

Chapter 2

1. As I was finishing this book, a colleague in Scotland, Sachi Arafat, kindly made me aware of "From the Philosophy of Information to the Philosophy of Information Culture" (Briggle and Mitcham 2009), which ends on the need for more research on the topic of friendship, as a special concern in the study of information culture.

Chapter 3

1. As one point, it is not clear that there is a distinct Cutter and Otlet tradition, at least in regard to Otlet's own works (it is notable that Balnaves and Willson's (2011) bibliography doesn't directly reference Otlet's works, but rather their work relies on secondary sources). There is not room in this book to develop this point further than to mention issues ranging from Otlet's mélange of philosophical sources and positions within and outside of documentation and librarianship to the fact of Otlet and LaFontaine's construction of the Universal Decimal Classification and other tools for document retrieval. Still, Balnaves and Willson's identification and discussions of two LIS traditions are important, no matter what proper names they have attached to them.

2. A more critical reading of the difference in these two traditions, and importantly, their epistemological, ontological, and methodological consequences from an LIS perspective can be found in Lai Ma's doctoral dissertation from Indiana University, Bloomington (Ma 2012).

3. However, see the Frohmann (1992) reading of ASK, to the contrary. I, too, in past publications agreed with Frohmann's perspective on Belkin's ASK, but more recently I have come to the conclusion that Belkin's texts do not well enough support such a reading.

4. The notion of "information" in LIS, however, remains contentious: see Jonathan Furner (2004) for his suggestion that the term isn't needed in information science to account for what it studies and what it does in professional practice. See also, for example, the work of Niels Windfeld Lund who has represented the neo-documentalist reaction to the information perspective in LIS.

Chapter 4

1. The article by Bernard Rieder (2012) is an extremely well-researched, concise article that examines the historical and the technical convergence of sociometrics, citation indexing and analysis, and network analysis in the sociotechnical functions of Google's PageRank algorithm.

2. Briet argued that documentation serves science, "like the dog on the hunt—totally before [the researcher], guided, guiding" (Briet 1954).

3. Documentary space resembles here the indexical relations of Judeo-Christian religious literary prefigurations (between the old and new testaments; see Auerbach 1957) and of Christian medieval iconography, in the latter case with flattened out spaces of representation and cosmologies of indexical references (Walsh 2012) cutting across and overlapping different temporal horizons, creating apocalyptic senses of returned identity in the future and of everlasting life for the dead. Perhaps this is

also where so much messianic hope and faith with the Internet and social networks and their visualizations lie, as well. Namely, a theological faith that beneath the mathematics of indexical mapping and complex network analyses there might be at least local, if not universal, truths about reality. And perhaps this is the reason why so many explanations and prognoses of such technologies resemble literary stories and why nodal network diagrams often resemble in their design medieval iconographic pictures of the saints.

4. The documentary universe, thus, may be taken as an allegory of life on earth. An allegory that has been reduced to realism by its insertion—as a constant explanatory and communicative presence—into our lives, like Christian iconography and tales were in medieval Europe.

5. From a skeptical perspective, over time modern technologies often seem to come to express the pathologies that lead them to appear in the first place. The Internet closes distances by means of computer mediation that in some ways increase our personal distance from one another. Airplanes that were built to narrow travel time end up requiring long waiting, boarding, and takeoff times, as their technologies of transportation are intricate, complex, and potentially dangerous, as well as quick. It could be proposed that psychotechnical pathologies are enfolded into modern technologies in their very design.

Chapter 5

1. But, we should also note that some language games involve, precisely, the breaking down of normative scripts—for example, avant-garde art activities in the twentieth century with their traditions of "shock" and defamiliarization—through a repertoire of techniques.

Chapter 6

1. See, among many other authors, the later works of Antonio Negri and, more generally, the Italian debate on "immaterial labor" (an English-language "sampler" of the Italian radical thought can be found in Virno and Hardt 1996). For more contemporary works, see among others, the many thoughtful works by Christian Fuchs.

2. As Ian Steadman, in a recent *Wired* (UK) article put it: "The big data approach to intelligence gathering allows an analyst to get the full resolution on worldwide affairs. Nothing is lost from looking too closely at one particular section of data; nothing is lost from trying to get too wide a perspective on a situation that the fine detail is lost. The algorithms find the patterns and the hypothesis follows from the data. The analyst doesn't even have to bother proposing a hypothesis any more. Her role switches from proactive to reactive, with the algorithms doing the contextual work. ... For science, it makes sense to see big data as a revolution. Algorithms will

spot patterns and generate theories, so there's a decreasing need to worry about inventing a hypothesis first and then testing it with a sample of data. ... In the same way that the internal combustion engine spelled the end of the horse as a working animal, big data could be the tool to render most of academic disciplines redundant if it proves better at building better narratives of human society" (Steadman 2013).

3. As Chris Anderson, writing for *Wired* in 2008, explained:

This is a world where massive amounts of data and applied mathematics replace every other tool that might be brought to bear. Out with every theory of human behavior, from linguistics to sociology. Forget taxonomy, ontology, and psychology. Who knows why people do what they do? The point is they do it, and we can track and measure it with unprecedented fidelity. With enough data, the numbers speak for themselves.

The big target here isn't advertising, though. It's science. The scientific method is built around testable hypotheses. These models, for the most part, are systems visualized in the minds of scientists. The models are then tested, and experiments confirm or falsify theoretical models of how the world works. This is the way science has worked for hundreds of years.

Scientists are trained to recognize that correlation is not causation, that no conclusions should be drawn simply on the basis of correlation between X and Y (it could just be a coincidence). Instead, you must understand the underlying mechanisms that connect the two. Once you have a model, you can connect the data sets with confidence. Data without a model is just noise.

But faced with massive data, this approach to science—hypothesize, model, test—is becoming obsolete. (Anderson 2008)

References

Althusser, L. (2001). Ideology and ideological state apparatus (notes towards an investigation). In *Lenin and Philosophy and other essays* (pp. 85–126). New York: Monthly Review Press.

Anderson, C. (2008, June 23). The end of theory: The data deluge makes the scientific method obsolete. *Wired*. http://archive.wired.com/science/discoveries/magazine /16-07/pb_theory.

Auerbach, E. (1957). Figura. (R. Manheim, Trans.). *Scenes from the drama of European literature*. New York: Meridian.

Baker, U. (2001). *What is opinion?* Television production. RedTV. Ankara, Turkey: Producer.

Balnaves, M., & Willson, M. (2011). *A new theory of information & the Internet*. New York: Peter Lang.

Belkin, N. J. (1977). Internal knowledge and external information. In *The Cognitive Viewpoint: Proceedings of an International Workshop on the Cognitive Point of View* (pp. 187–194). Ghent, Netherlands: University of Ghent.

Benjamin, W. (1968). The work of art in the age of mechanical reproduction. In H. Arendt (Ed.), *Illuminations* (pp. 217–251). (Zohn, H., Trans.). New York: Schocken.

Berardi, F. (2001). *La fabbrica dell'infelicità: new economy e movimento del cognitariato*. Rome: DeriveApprodi.

Blanchette, J. F., & Johnson, D. G. (2002). Data retention and the panoptic society: The social benefits of forgetfulness. *Information Society*, 18, 33–45.

Bollen, J., Goncalves, B., Ruan, G., & Mao, H. (2011). Happiness is assortative in online social networks. *Artificial Life*, 17(3), 237–251.

Bollen, J., Mao, H., & Zeng, X. (2011). Twitter mood predicts the stock market. *Journal of Computational Science*, 2(1), 1–8.

Bowker, G. (2005). *Memory practices in the sciences*. Cambridge, MA: MIT Press.

Bowker, G., & Star, S. L. (1999). *Sorting things out: Classification and its consequences.* Cambridge, MA: MIT Press.

Briet, S. (1951). *Qu'est-ce que la documentation?* Paris: Édit/Éditions Documentaires.

Briet, S. (1954). Bibliothécaires et documentalistes. *Revue de documentation* (21), 41–45.

Briet, S. (2006). *What is documentation?: English translation of the classic French text.* Translated and edited by Ronald E. Day and Laurent Martinet, with Hermina G. B. Anghelescu. Lanham, MD: Scarecrow Press.

Briggle, A., & Mitcham, C. (2009). From the philosophy of information to the philosophy of information culture. *Information Society, 25*(3), 169–174.

Brown, J. S., & Duguid, P. (2000). *The social life of information.* Boston: Harvard Business School Press.

Buckland, M. K. (1991). Information as thing. *Journal of the American Society for Information Science American Society for Information Science, 42*(5), 351–360.

Buckland, M. K. (1997). What is a document? *Journal of the American Society for Information Science American Society for Information Science, 48*(9), 804–809.

Buckland, M. K. (1998). What is a "digital document"? *Document Numérique* (Paris), *2*(2), 221–230.

Buckland, M. K. (2012a, June 1, 2012).Personal communication.

Buckland, M. K. (2012b). What kind of science *can* information science be? *Journal of the American Society for Information Science and Technology, 63*(1), 1–7.

Coleridge, S. T. (1984). *Biographia literaria* (Vol. 7). Princeton: Princeton University Press.

Cowley, S. J. & MacDorman, K. F. (2006). What baboons, babies, and Tetris players tell us about interaction: a biosocial view of norm-based social learning. *Connection Science, 18*(4), 363–378.

Cronin, B. (1984). *The citation process: The role and significance of citations in scientific communication.* London: Taylor Graham.

Day, R. E. (2001). *The modern invention of information: Discourse, history, and power.* Carbondale: Southern Illinois University Press.

Day, R. E. (2006). "A necessity of our time": Documentation as "cultural technique". In *What is documentation?: English translation of the classic French text* (pp. 46–63). Lanham, MD: Scarecrow Press.

Day, R. E. (2007). Knowing and indexical psychology. In C. McInerney & R. E. Day (Eds.), *Rethinking knowledge management: From knowledge artifacts to knowledge processes* (pp. 331–348). Berlin: Springer.

Day, R. E. (2011). Death of the user: Reconceptualizing subjects, objects, and their relations. *Journal of the American Society for Information Science and Technology, 62*(1), 78–88.

Day, R. E. (2013). "The data—it is me!" ("Les données—c'est moi'!). In B. C. Cronin and C. R. Sugimoto (Eds.), *Beyond bibliometrics: Harnessing multidimensional indicators of scholarly impact* (pp. 67–84). Cambridge, MA: MIT Press.

Deleuze, G. (1990). *The logic of sense* (M. L. C. Stivale, Trans.). New York: Columbia University Press.

Deleuze, G. (1995). *Postscript on control societies negotiations* (pp. 177–182). New York: Columbia University Press.

Drucker, J. (2013). *What is? Nine epistemological essays*. Victoria, TX: Cuneiform Press.

Duhigg, C. (2012, June 16). How companies learn your secrets. *New York Times*. http://www.nytimes.com/2012/02/19/magazine/shopping-habits.html.

Edwards, P. N. (2010). *A vast machine: Computer models, climate data, and the politics of global warming*. Cambridge, MA: MIT Press.

Ekbia, H. (2008). *Artificial dreams: The quest for non-biological intelligence*. Cambridge: Cambridge University Press.

Enright, N. F. (2013). The violence of information literacy: Neoliberalism and the human as capital. In L. G. S. Higgins (Ed.), *Information Literacy and Social Justice: Radical Professional Praxis* (pp. 15–38). Sacramento, CA: Library Juice Press.

Fayet-Scribe, S. (2000). *Histoire de la documentation en France culture, science et technologie de l'information: 1895–1937*. Paris: CNRS-Éditions.

Fortunati, L. (1995). *The arcane of reproduction: Housework, prostitution, labor and capital* (H. Creek, Trans.). Brooklyn, NY: Automedia.

Foucault, M. (2008). *The Birth of Biopolitics: Lectures at the Collège de France, 1978–1979* (G. Burchell, Trans.). New York: Palgrave Macmillan.

Frege, G. (1952). On sense and reference. In P. T. G. M. Black (Ed.), *Translations from the Philosophical Writings of Gottlob Frege* (pp. 56–78). Oxford: Oxford University Press.

Freud, S. (1959). The "uncanny." In *Collected papers* (vol. 4, pp. 368–407). New York: Basic Books.

Frohmann, B. (1992). The power of images: A discourse analysis of the cognitive viewpoint. *Journal of Documentation, 48*(4), 365–386.

Frohmann, B. (2004). *Deflating information: From science studies to documentation*. Toronto: University of Toronto Press.

Furner, J. (2004). Information studies without information. *Library Trends, 52*(3), 427–446.

Gadamer, H.-G. (2004). *Truth and method* (J. Weinsheimer and D. G. Marshall, Trans. 2nd ed.). New York: Crossroad.

Guizzo, E. (2010). Geminoid F gets job as robot actress. *IEEE Spectrum*. http://spec trum.ieee.org/automaton/robotics/humanoids/geminoid-f-takes-the-stage.

Harré, R. (1989). The "self" as a theoretical concept. In M. Krausz (Ed.), *Relativism: Interpretation and confrontation* (pp. 387–417). Notre Dame, IN: Notre Dame University Press.

Harvey, D. (2005). *A brief history of neoliberalism*. New York: Oxford University Press.

Hayles, N. K. (2012). *How we think: Digital media and contemporary technogenesis*. Chicago: University of Chicago Press.

Hegel, G. W. F. (1977). *Phenomenology of spirit* (A. V. Miller, Trans.). Oxford: Clarendon.

Heidegger, M. (1962). *Being and time*. New York: Harper & Row.

Heidegger, M. (1977a). The age of the world picture. In D. F. Krell (Ed.), *Martin Heidegger: Basic writings from Being and Time (1927) to the Task of Thinking (1964)* (pp. 115–154). New York: Harper & Row.

Heidegger, M. (1977b). The end of philosophy and the task of thinking. In D. F. Krell (Ed.), *Martin Heidegger: Basic writings from Being and Time (1927) to the Task of Thinking (1964)* (pp. 373–392). New York: Harper & Row.

Issenberg, S. (2012, December 16). How President Obama's campaign used big data to rally individual voters, part 1. *MIT Technology Review*.

Jameson, F. (1982). *The political unconscious: Narrative as a socially symbolic act*. Ithaca, NY: Cornell University Press.

Jentsch, E. (1996). On the psychology of the uncanny. *Angelaki, 2*(1), 7–16.

Kant, I. (2000). *Critique of the power of judgment* (P. Guyer, Trans.). Cambridge: Cambridge University Press.

Kant, I. (2009). *An answer to the question: What is enlightenment?* New York: Penguin.

Lacan, J. (2006). The mirror stage as formative of the *I* function as revealed in psychoanalytic experience. In *Écrits* (pp. 75–81). New York: Norton.

Lund, N. W. (2009). Document theory. *Annual Review of Information Science & Technology, 43*, 399–432.

Ma, L. (2012). Information in our world: Conceptions of information and problems of method in information science. Ph.D. dissertation. Bloomington: Indiana University.

MacDorman, K. F., & Cowley, S. J. (2006). Long-term relationships as a benchmark for robot personhood. Paper presented at the 15th IEEE International Symposium on Robot and Human Interactive Communication, University of Hertfordshire, Hatfield, UK.

MacDorman, K. F., & Ishiguro, H. (2006). The uncanny advantage of using androids in cognitive and social science research. *Interaction Studies: Social Behaviour and Communication in Biological and Artificial Systems, 7*(3), 297–337.

MacDorman, K. F., Vasudevan, S. K., & Ho, C.-C. (2009). Does Japan really have robot mania? Comparing attitudes by implicit and explicit measures. *AI & Society, 23*(4), 485–510.

Marazzi, C. (2008). *Capital and language: From the new economy to the war economy.* Los Angeles: Semiotext(e).

Marx, K. [1865] (1969). *Value, price and profit.* New York: International Co., Inc.

Marx, K. (1977). *Capital* (B. Fowkes, Trans.). Vol. 1. New York: Vintage.

Mori, M. (2012). The uncanny valley [Bukimi no Tani Genshō]. (Trans. Karl F. MacDorman and Norri Kageki). *IEEE Robotics & Automation Magazine, 19*(2), 98–100.

Oh, H. (2010, November 18). Japan robot takes the stage, stiffly. *Reuters.* http://www.reuters.com/article/2010/11/18/us-japan-robot-idUSTRE6AH2YB20101118.

Otlet, P. (1934). *Traité de documentation: le livre sur le livre: Théorie et pratique.* Brussels: Editiones Mundaneum, Palais Mondial.

Otlet, P. (1935). *Monde: Essai d'universalisme: Connaissance du monde, sentiment du monde, action organisée et plan du monde.* Brussels: Éditiones Mundaneum.

Otlet, P. (Ed.). (1990). *International organisation and dissemination of knowledge: Selected essays of Paul Otlet.* Amsterdam: Elsevier.

Rayward, W. B. (1975). *The universe of information: The work of Paul Otlet for documentation and international organisation.* Moscow: VINITI.

Rayward, W. B. (1994). Visions of Xanadu: Pault Otlet (1868–1944) and hypertext. *Journal of the American Society for Information Science, 45*(4), 235–250.

Reddy, M. J. (1979). The conduit metaphor: A case of frame conflict in our language about language. In A. Ortony (Ed.), *Metaphor and thought* (pp. 284–310). Cambridge: Cambridge University Press.

Reich, R. B. (1992). *The work of nations: Preparing ourselves for 21st century capitalism.* New York: Vintage Books.

Rieder, B. (2012). What is in PageRank? A historical and conceptual investigation of a recursive status index. *Computational Culture*. http://computationalculture.net/article/what_is_in_pagerank.

Ronell, A. (2005). *The test drive*. Urbana: University of Illinois Press.

Rouvroy, A. (2013). The end(s) of critique: data-behaviourism vs. due-process. In M. Hildebrandt & K. de Vries (Ed.), *Privacy, due process and the computational turn: The philosophy of law meets the philosophy of technology*. New York: Routledge.

Šabanović, S. (2010). Emotion in robot cultures: Cultural models of affect in social robot design. Paper presented at the Design and Emotion Conference 2010, Chicago.

Saussure, F., Baskin, W., Meisel, P., & Saussy, H. (2011). *Course in general linguistics*. New York: Columbia University Press.

Sengers, P. (2002). Narrative and schizophrenia in artifical agents. *Leonardo, 35*(2), 427–431.

Small, H. G. (1978). Cited documents as concept symbols. *Social Studies of Science, 8*(3), 327–340.

Steadman, I. (2013, January 25). Big data and the death of the theorist. http://www.wired.co.uk/news/archive/2013-01/25/big-data-end-of-theory.

Terranova, T. (2004). *Network culture: politics for the information age*. London: Pluto Press.

Thomas, N. (2011). Social computing as social rationality. Ph.D. dissertation, McGill University, Montreal, Canada.

Thomas, N. (2012). Algorithmic subjectivity and the need to be in-formed. Paper presented at the TEM 2012: First Conference Proceedings of the Technology and Emerging Media Track, Canadian Communication Association conference, Kitchener-Waterloo, Ontario. http://www.tem.fl.ulaval.ca/en/waterloo-2012.

Turkle, S. (2011). *Alone together: Why we expect more from technology and less from each other*. New York: Basic Books.

Virno, P., & Hardt, M. (1996). *Radical thought in Italy: A potential politics*. Minneapolis: University of Minnesota Press.

Walsh, J. A. (2012). "Images of God and friends of God": The holy icon as document. *Journal of the American Society for Information Science and Technology, 63*(1), 185–194.

Wiener, N. (1954). *The human use of human beings: Cybernetics and society*. New York: Houghton.

Wiener, N. (1961). *Cybernetics: or control and communicaqtion in the animal and the machine* (2nd ed.). Cambridge, MA: MIT Press.

Wilson, P. (1983). *Second-hand knowledge. An inquiry into cognitive authority.* Westport, CT: Greenwood Press.

Yates, J. (1989). *Control through communication: The rise of system in American management.* Baltimore: Johns Hopkins University Press.

Index